Mysticism

Window on a
World View

Margaret Lewis Furse

ABINGDON
Nashville

Mysticism: Window on a World View

Copyright © 1977 by Abingdon

Library of Congress Cataloging in Publication Data

FURSE, MARGARET LEWIS.
  Mysticism, window on a world view.
  Includes bibliographical references and index.
  1. Mysticism. I. Title.
          BL625.F87   291.4′2   76-56816

ISBN 0-687-27674-8

Portions of chapter 6 appeared originally in "The Mystical and the Personal in Emil Brunner and Baron von Hügel," *Rice University Studies,* 60 (Winter, 1974), pp. 1-20.

The poem "Ideal" by Sister Mary Agnes on page 16 is reprinted from *Anglican Theological Review,* LVII (January 1975), p. 105.

Selections from *Meister Eckhart: A Modern Translation* by Raymond Bernard Blakney, copyright, 1941 by Harper & Row, Publishers, Inc., and an abridgment of a chart on page 79 in *Apology for Wonder* by Sam Keen, copyright © 1969 by Sam Keen, are reprinted by permission of Harper & Row, Publishers, Inc.

Scripture quotations unless otherwise noted are from the Revised Standard Version of the Bible, copyrighted 1946, 1952, © 1971, 1973.

MANUFACTURED BY THE PARTHENON PRESS AT
NASHVILLE, TENNESSEE, UNITED STATES OF AMERICA

To
  Janie
  Austen
  John and
  Mary

Preface

This short preface is intended to express my great thanks. My sense of gratitude is too pervasive to be counted up in debts of gratitude, and all my thanking is bound to be a poor return for the bounty I have received. I think it has been the special quality of my parents' generosity to have given not only gifts, but more, a liberation from all claims to recompense. Freedom and a general disposition toward happiness are no small gifts to have received. I hope I can learn how to give them, too, and learn, as well, how to say or make or live an effective thanks. One day, if a bookish approach to personal ethics does not seem inappropriate, I would like to try to describe the theoretical ingredients and moral dilemmas of generosity and gratitude. Until then, let me express my sincere thanks as adequately as I can.

I am grateful to my parents, friends, and to many former teachers at Columbia University and Union Theological Seminary. For the encouragement and opportunity to teach, I am indebted to Niels C. Nielsen, Jr., chairman of Rice Unversity's Department of Religious Studies. I would like to thank Gilbert Douglas, with whom I worked for several years as a teaching partner at Rice in a course on mysticism and existentialism. Having moved with my family to Austin, I have now been taken into the stimulating company of William H. Goetzmann, Robert M. Crunden, William Stott, Elspeth Rostow, and David Hovland in the American Studies program at the University of Texas. There, in the spirit of "Farewell

Eckhart, hail Thoreau," I have been teaching a course on mysticism in America.

For a great deal of helpful critical advice on the manuscript, I would like to single out for special thanks James Sellers of Rice University and the late Stuart Currie of Austin Presbyterian Seminary. And I wish to thank Laura L. Knight for an expert job in the typing of many drafts.

Finally and always, I have my husband to thank for so often recalling my vagrant attention to four subjects of greater interest, which are, however, not unrelated to this book; they are our children, delightful companions, to whom with love and gratitude it is dedicated.

Margaret Lewis Furse

Contents

PART ONE: DEFINITIONS

PART TWO: SOURCES

PART THREE: INTERPRETATIONS

Introduction

In this book, two main tasks have been set before us. One is the need to say what mysticism is—to introduce mysticism to the general reader of a more or less philosophical turn of mind. The need to do so is especially evident today because that vague word "mysticism" is daily being made even more vague by its unlimited application to every sort of religious phenomenon and cult. Included in one of the best brief treatments of mysticism was the following statement by William Ernest Hocking:

> On account of its common uses, the name "mysticism" is more misleading than any other of our type-names. As a form of philosophy, mysticism is not to be associated with occultism or superstition, nor with psychical research, nor with an application of the fourth dimension to psychology, nor with a cult of vagueness, nor with a special love of the mysterious for its own sake. (*Types of Philosophy* [New York: Charles Scribner's Sons, 1929], p. 255; cf. chaps. 33, 34, 35, 36)

If this vagueness was evident when Hocking wrote in 1929, it is positively epidemic now. Today if the average person were asked what mysticism is, he would surely put on his list many of the very items Hocking excluded from his. The source of the irony is not hard to find. Hocking was speaking of mysticism as a type of *philosophy*. What commands popular attention today are cults, religious movements, and practices—the *visible*

13

social expression of strange religions. The tools of the sociologist are necessary for the important task of investigating these phenomena. But in this book we, like Hocking, are primarily concerned to say what mysticism is, not as a social movement, but as a world view: What is its estimate of reality? What is the nature of knowledge and of the moral life that that world view implies? Is there a general pattern to mysticism—dimly discernible in some examples, more pronounced in others? Grappling with such questions is not primarily an empirical undertaking, but it cannot fail to be an inquiry of interest and assistance to the empirical worker.

Our second main aim in this book is to elucidate Christian mysticism. How can Christian mysticism be described against the backdrop of Eastern mysticism? What are some of its historical roots? What do two representative Christian mystics say for themselves? How has Christian mysticism been interpreted in the past? And, finally, what is the chief theological issue for Christianity when it considers mysticism?

It would be reassuring if we could simply indicate by a label or some one-sentence definition what mysticism is and what this book about mysticism is about. But when the subject is vast (and mysticism is a vast subject), the brevity essential to labels plays tricks with telling the whole truth. Understandably, the first noise made by writers and readers of vast subjects is a whimper. Happily, in the present case, there is a comforting thought for both. Labels, even though misleading, have their usefulness, and while it is true that mysticism is a vast subject, this is not a vast book.

What is mysticism? Most briefly, mysticism is the recovery of immediacy. If we were pasting on a space-saving label, that is how it would read. The mystic is one who believes that immediacy can be recovered and who has some experience of doing so himself. The word "immediacy" here can be described in three types of metaphor, but basically it is a denial of some kind of separation.

In the metaphor of space, immediacy is expressed as being *at one* with God (or whatever is named the deepest reality). God is here, not merely there. In the metaphor of time, immediacy means that God is present. No interval of time separates the mystic and God. His experience of God does not lie in the past or the future; it is now. In the metaphor of manner, immediacy is the spontaneity that removes in a flash all studied and effortful means or techniques of approaching God. Immediate knowledge does not wait for the gathering of evidence, nor does innocence need to plan a strategy for goodness.

The great religious motivation of the mystic is to recover that original state of oneness from which we are apparently (though the mystic assumes not really) separated. What might the story of separation and recovery mean in everyday life?

Act 1: Separation. So long as one assumes a separation one is in a state of disquiet. The mind is at work puzzling over intellectual problems. What is truth? Does God exist? The sensibilities are alert to moral dilemmas. What ought I to do? These busy intellectual and moral efforts are not judged by the mystic as valueless; they are seen as a preliminary to something more ultimate toward which he desires to move. They are like act 1 of a two-act play. In act 1 there is separation and disquiet; in act 2 reunion, recovery, and quietude.

Act 2: Recovery. The recovery of immediacy will mean, then, a relaxation of both discursive intellectual activity and moral effort. Now the mystic knows at first hand that which he could only puzzle over before. And now without any effort of the will he does what he "ought" to do and has no need to make moral distinctions. "Passivity" is the descriptive word often used of this more ultimate stage. "Peace" might be better. "Union" is the common word of Christian mysticism; "enlightenment," though by no means equivalent, is its Eastern approximation.

A recent poem entitled "Ideal," by Sister Mary Agnes, an English nun of the Order of Poor Clares, serves nicely as a kind of personal synopsis of this story of separation and recovery. She writes—

> Do you aspire
> to some form of beauty
> you can never acquire?
>   I do too
> I have stormed weary nights
> in quest of it
> torn petals apart,
> desperate
> then suddenly discovered
> I have it already
> here with me
> now.

In a more pedestrian way, we can here summarize acts 1 and 2 and indicate the changes they reflect in everyday life:

Preliminary Act 1: SEPARATION	Ultimate Act 2: RECOVERY
Being distant from God	Being at one with God
God "was" or "shall be"	Enjoying the presence of God
Knowing God through some intellectual means (proofs)	Immediate knowledge of God
Needing moral effort; puzzling over ethical distinctions. Needing training in discipline and technique.	Enjoying moral innocence; needing no moral distinctions or efforts.

It is important to say that the mystic's enterprise (i.e., his world view and what he does about it) consists of these two stages—a preliminary and an ultimate (act 1 and act 2)—because it will help make apparent why a simple list of the characteristics of mysticism is somewhat misleading. Whatever one says of act 2 (which is relatively passive), one cannot simply say of act 1 (which is relatively active). That is why in this book we refer to a *pattern* of mysticism—a pattern with a motion like drama or choreography, not a pattern like a mosaic. First there is a twoness, a separation that gives rise to disquiet; then there is reunion and quietude. Both stages are part of the pattern, but certainly the mystic's aim is act 2, the recovery of immediacy. It must also be added that "ultimate" does not simply mean the last thing done or the last stage achieved in a literal temporal sense. In actual life act 1 and act 2 may be played again and again. Ordinary day-to-day moral and intellectual efforts (of act 1) can be invested with a joy that derives from the reminiscence and anticipation of act 2. Commonly the mystic returns to the everyday and finds it hallowed. The mystic of the East can return to the world of samsara and experience it as Nirvana.

We can, then, label mysticism as "the recovery of immediacy," and with some misgivings suggest the following list of the contents indicated by that label.

Characteristics of Mysticism

1. NATURE OF REALITY: A SEEMING TWONESS, A REAL ONENESS
    Reality is one and lies beyond all apparent divisions. It is, in ordinary words, *indescribable*. Our apparent separation from it gives rise to spiritual disquiet, which evidences *the self's essential kinship with it*. Despite its ineffability and our apparent separation from it, we can attain an *intuitive knowledge* of it and a *moral harmony* with it. Self-knowledge gives access to it; access to it gives self-knowledge.

2. PRACTICE: A PRELIMINARY ACTIVE DISCIPLINE; AN ULTIMATE PASSIVITY (PEACE, UNION, ENLIGHTENMENT)
    Some discipline or asceticism is necessary as a preliminary, and much of the writing of the mystics is

concerned with their disciplinary recommendations. Ultimately, efforts of mind and will relax. Disciplinary efforts of the first stage are now either no longer needed or are accomplished without effort.

The following characteristics of mysticism are more strictly speaking characteristics of the ultimate stage:

3.   KNOWLEDGE: INTUITIVE, NONDISCURSIVE
     In mysticism there is an implied criticism of ordinary ways of knowing. When one has recovered immediacy of intuitive knowing, one discards piecemeal knowing.

4.   ETHICS: ETHICAL INDIFFERENTISM
     Moral distinctions and effort are no longer necessary. God (or Reality) is a One that lies beyond such distinctions.

5.   TIME: A PREFERENCE FOR PRESENT TIME
     The focus is on the "now" and its present experience, not on the past or future.

This book is by no means an exhaustive study of the general subject of mysticism, nor is it a piece of empirical work in the history of religion. This is more a book of ideas, suggestions, and interpretations than of definitions and exact descriptions. What is said to the reader is, "Try thinking of mysticism this way and see if the pattern seems to fit most of the examples you meet." The warning on the label reads, "Caution! These suggestions may not always work. Special handling may be needed in certain cases." What we have here is an hypothesis, an essay, a working description—a label with a question mark. The details presented in this book are there for the sake of elucidating an hypothesis, not for the sake of proving it.

PART ONE
Definitions

From Alan W. Watts's dedication to *The Way of Zen:*
　To Tia, Mark, and Richard who will understand it all the better for not being able to read it.

From R. H. Blyth's dedication of *Zen and Zen Classics:*
　Dedicated as all my books shall be to Suzuki Daisetz who taught me all that I don't know.

From *The New York Times Magazine,* July 26, 1970:
　The golf swing is now entering a new era: the mystical. Amateurs have always suspected that there is something about it that the pros know and won't reveal. Hence the books on the "magic" moves in golf, and the "secret" of swing. . . . Alex Morrison anticipated the New Mysticisms three decades ago when he advocated an entirely new approach . . . : just don't practice.

Chapter 1
Mysticism, Not Mystical Experience

Mysticism, as a way of thinking and acting, is more likely than any other religious orientation to be either embraced or rejected uncritically. Ironically, it is both the detractors and the advocates who dismiss the possibility of a critical treatment of mysticism. Both sides merely react; it is only a question of whether with favor or disfavor. It is true that in a debate mysticism is never entered in the lists; it does not follow that mysticism, as a subject, has nothing to offer thoughtful, discursive inquiry.

What is needed is a critical view, an appraisal of mysticism that puts some distance between the appraiser and the subject, a view that involves recognizing the difficulties and aberrations as well as the promise of mysticism. Mysticism has often been studied in terms of devotional life, less often as a pattern of thought and practice. The point of view of this book is that whatever the difficulty may be of dealing with an uncommon way of knowing, the intellectual and ethical problems manifest in mysticism are as instructive for Christian thought as mystical feeling is promising for Christian devotion. It is, in this writer's opinion, a singularly arid and unprofitable approach to mysticism to seek to authenticate mystical experience itself. Critical study of mysticism is not a matter of accepting, rejecting, or in some way validating the mystical experience; it is a matter of understanding what pattern of thought and action is adopted if one tends toward that type of religion called "mystical."

Mysticism Today

Our time appears to be one of particular susceptibility to mysticism, not as a doctrine or historical phenomenon, but as a mood and a practice. These are times in which new experiences are siezed and then afterwards described—if indeed they are described at all. To assess, to trace historical roots, to examine before tasting, seems too prudent and too timid. Astrology, Theosophy, Scientology, Zen, Satanism, Subud, Hare Krishna, Transcendental Meditation (TM), the Children of God, Pentecostalism—these names represent some of the opportunities for the popular religious experimenting that is going on today. Week by week on any college campus a new religious group, guru, or meditative technique is announced on a placard. "You're trying out religions the way other people try boxes of cereal," teased one professor. "Yes," came the student's reply, "but I always learn something from each one." Students are not the only ones doing the experimenting. The title of an article on Transcendental Meditation in *Psychology Today* shows its general appeal: "If Well-Integrated but Anxious, Try TM."[1] And in a recent article for the *New York Times Magazine,* Andrew Greeley posed the question, "Are We a Nation of Mystics?"[2] By no means are all these new religious orientations types of mysticism. There appears, however, to be a growing tolerance—and even a preference—for what is irrational, for private experience, for the occult, and for drug-induced states. There may be developing, therefore, a new popular openness toward whatever is irrational and, insofar as mysticism is to be interpreted as irrational, toward mysticism.

If times past are any indication of the present, then our susceptibility to the mood of mysticism is due not only to a potentially irrational component in mysticism but to a disaffection with old religious doctrines and institutions. Mysticism, at least partly, is a reaction of reform *against* stultifying religious dogma and *in favor of* a "direct religious experience" that is "living" and "personal."[3] Perhaps our time is like the period of Catholic Modernism, in which the interest in mysticism in the early part of the twentieth century increased in direct proportion to the demise of biblical literalism. When old thought-forms, old practices fail to inspire, mysticism is embraced.

In our day, this is especially true. Perhaps this openness to mysticism is partly due to the deep-seated disillusionment with the little that step-by-step, discursive reason—in its philosophical, technological, or political applications—has been able to achieve. The British journalist Malcolm Muggeridge expressed the current disenchantment with technological know-how in an especially vivid way. In his book *Jesus Rediscovered,* he shows more than a tinge of the mystic's otherworldliness:

> In a way, it's deliriously funny, of course—going to the moon when you can't walk with safety through Central Park, or for that matter through Hyde Park nowadays, after dark; fixing up a middle-aged dentist with a new heart in one part of Africa while in another part tens of thousands die of starvation in a squalid tribal war for which we, among others, provide arms; promoting happiness enriched by an ever-rising Gross National Product, and sanctified by birth pills, pot, and abortions for all on the National Health, while the psychiatric wards fill to overflowing, suicides multiply, and crimes of violence increase year by year.[4]

Nor does there appear to Muggeridge to be any basis for confidence in the techniques of politics or social welfare.

> The prevailing notion is that salvation can come only through action, and that whatever deflects our attention from here and now is an evasion, a selfish pursuit of private virtue and serenity. Yet think of all the Kingdoms of

heaven on earth that have been proclaimed in our time.
Where are they now? [The Reich, Stalin's paradise on
earth, The Welfare State, the Great Society]—the bottom's
fallen out of all of them, hasn't it?[5]

Today, too, there is a monumental disillusionment
with discursive reason in the form of the Protestant
Ethic—the intramundane asceticism of hard work,
sobriety, and prudence, earning one's way by chipping at
one's work, waiting one's turn according to the tables of
seniority—all this is called into question. What is
popularly summarized in the phrase "Protestant Ethic"
and what is currently questioned, is a *piecemeal*
approach to life. The present cry is to embrace life in its
whole, to see life (or truth or the "meaningful"—
whatever the current phrase) in one vision—not frag-
mented into various occupations and duties. Here is the
very point at which mysticism with its vision of the
"One" or its promise of satori makes itself congenial to
our times. Leaving the piecemeal, mysticism yearns for a
single vision. It is especially important today to ask what
is the nature of that vision and what relation, if any, it has
toward the piecemeal.

There appears to be a new popular interest in oriental
religions and their practices, but less interest in Christian mysticism. One reason, as J. H. Randall points out in
The Role of Knowledge in Western Religion is that
Western religion has been fraught with doctrinal squab-
bles in a way that the Eastern religions, which take a
more practical approach, have largely escaped. Westerners "hardly realize how distinctively Christian and
indeed Protestant" has been the problem of faith and
knowledge. "No other culture has assigned so central a
place to religious beliefs." For Judaism and Islam the
question is not so much of doctrine as of following the
law; for Buddhism and Hinduism, religion is a path of
life; for Confucians, a standard of conduct. "The Oriental
religions have indeed been very practical, concentrating
on conduct and behavior. They all take religion, not as a

set of beliefs to be accepted as theoretically true . . . but as a life to be lived, a path to be trodden."[6]

This practical rather than doctrinal orientation in Eastern religions makes them amenable to the modern Western mind, which, however disillusioned with technology, is nevertheless too practical to find itself torn over a narrow theological question of whether the relationship between God the Father and God the Son is better expressed as *homoousios* or *homoiousios*. It seems much more productive, in a way, simply to experiment with assuming the Lotus position to see if such meditations "work."

The current temper is very well described and criticized by Sam Keen in *Apology for Wonder*. There he describes modern man as a practical-minded doer—a *homo faber*. *"Homo faber* became a central image of modern man as a direct result of the collapse of belief in the creative and informing power of a transcendent God. If God, cosmic reason, or any surrogate for these traditional divinities does not give life meaning, then man himself must take over the task."[7] Eastern religions—especially Zen, which is now enjoying a vogue—give the practical-minded, disillusioned Westerner a program with which he can be free to experiment and one that seems to him at least to be free of doctrinal encrustations that offend his conscience.

The mystical element in religion—the contemplative, the passive—has not, since the Reformation at least, been a primary conscious emphasis of the Christian church. The ethic of the churches has been less an aesthetic than a social and activist ethic. Make a difference in *this* world. Build hospitals. Give to the poor. But the disillusioned can see that these efforts have been less than totally successful—and one thing that characterizes the expectations of our times is that successes be total. Withdrawal from society has some suasion.

Our calendars push and squeeze us until we have no time to feel, make love, delight in the beauty of the world, smell

flowers, play. We are all too uptight and money-mad. But
here there comes an important difference. For the flower
people there is no need to struggle for power. The society is
putrified within and will soon topple of its own accord. . . .
So [the flower children] like the first Franciscans, . . . walk
the streets in happy poverty conversing with the birds and
angering the sensible, thrifty pillars of the society.[8]

Either withdrawal or absolute apocalyptical victory
over evils, this is the appeal today; and the basis of the
appeal is disillusionment with a piecemeal way of doing
things, a disillusionment that rejects an ethic of building
brick by brick and a method of thought that proceeds
discursively, step by step. It is immediacy of result that is
required, and immediacy can be bestowed either passively by withdrawal *now* or militantly by confrontation
now.

There appears to be developing an odd merger
between apocalypticism and mysticism. The thing that
the "high noon" confrontation and mystical withdrawal
have in common is the insistence on the now—a
rejection of chronological time. With characteristic
verve, Harvey Cox describes the merger in his chapter
"Mystics and Militants" in *Feast of Fools*. The militant's
tactic "is not withdrawal but confrontation. Instead of
'turn on and drop out,' they prefer to 'sit in and take
over.'" But, as Cox points out, mystics and militants have
a good deal in common—especially in contrast to the
larger culture they both criticize. "Both agree that a
fundamental change is needed in society and that such a
change cannot be accomplished merely through normal
political channels. Both strongly emphasize the inner
voice of conscience as the final arbiter in moral affairs."[9]

Protestant activism together with the theologians'
charge of "depersonalizing" have foreclosed mysticism
as a central emphasis in the Protestant form of
Christianity. The Catholic tradition, too, has partaken of
the activist Protestant Ethic, and at the same time it has
too often interpreted mysticism in the special devotional
language of its own rich heritage, that is, as a rare

experience of the cloistered, gifted, and celibate religious specialist. Suddenly, at a time when contemplative values have great popular appeal, the church itself is bereft of advice to give. The former Archbishop of Canterbury, Dr. Michael Arthur Ramsey, has put the problem at the door of the church. "We haven't emphasized enough the role of contemplation in Christian life so people are finding it in non-Christian movements."[10] The time is ripe for a popular appreciation of the mystical tradition, but the Christian church, whose attention has been on doctrine and social activism, has been caught without an inventory of its spiritual treasury.

Obstacles in Approaching Mysticism

The first problem is how to go about thinking critically about mysticism when the word "mysticism" itself announces to common sense more forcefully than anything else that what is being discussed is in some sense irrational and unthinkable. Whether this impression is wholly justified is an important question that, for the moment, must be deferred because it hinges on an even larger one. That question is the nature of reason itself and hence the nature of the irrational.

It does seem true, however, that mysticism is different in character from that of a stated position with which one might agree or disagree. This difference—call it an irrational character if you will ("nondiscursive" character is preferred here)—means that one's reaction to mysticism, or whatever is referred to by that word, is conditioned by how one evaluates a nondiscursive kind of thing. Some persons—representatives of linguistic analysis, for example—think of anything "religious" as nonrational and, therefore, "mystical." If one happens to think that everything *should* be discursive, then whatever is mystical will be rejected. A. J. Ayer presents us with a clear example of this point of view. When theists assert that God "cannot be proved," he says, "they may mean that God is the object of a purely mystical intuition and cannot therefore be defined in terms which are intelligible to reason." But "to say that something transcends the understanding is to say it is unintelligible and cannot be significantly described." It must follow, complains Ayer, that "if a mystic admits that the object of his vision is something which cannot be described, then he must also admit that he is bound to talk nonsense when he describes it."[11] Thus, in approaching mysticism, we need to be prepared to do some thinking about such terms as *rational* and *irrational*.

Another obstacle to a critical study of mysticism is put in our way by those to whom being "religious" is to be morally assertive, politically involved, and socially active. To be "mystical" suggests disengagement and withdrawal from problem-solving activity and, therefore, from useful service. Something of this pattern of thought is at work in the tax laws of Great Britain, which permit a tax exemption for active religious orders of monks and nuns but no exemption for the purely contemplative orders. Here the criterion that must be met is socially useful activity. Who can fail to regard with utter seriousness the undeniable truth that contemplation in itself does not feed hungry mouths. And who is not put off by the possibility that contemplation can degenerate into a program of self-cultivation that, however "spiritual," can become altogether self-centered. But in the life of the mystic himself, when on one side of the scales are put the practical priorities—politics, strategy and tactics, and all the managerial skills—and on the other side the mystic's vision, how surely in his own view will vision outweigh technique! And how quickly will he put his own techniques in the service of his vision!

Just this viewpoint will make the mystic seem to be flying from this world rather than dealing with it, here and now. To be "mystical," then, can suggest the moral irresponsibility that attends otherworldliness. Again, the justification for this impression is a large question hinging on one still larger—the question of the best analogy (not a *scale* surely!) for understanding the relationship between "this world" and "that world."

A third obstacle looms so large in Christian mysticism that we need to deal with it at some length. It is the suspicion on the part of some Christian thinkers that the *mystical* and the *personal* are antithetical terms.

The Mystical and the Personal

That mysticism is essentially "de-personalizing" has been the conviction of several strands of Protestant theology. First of all, the ethical emphasis of Ritschl, Harnack, and the so-called Liberal theologians led to a search for an accurate picture of the historical Jesus, so that "personal" religion was interpreted not as a relationship with a "Thou" but as a personal achievement, an emulation of the moral example of Jesus, which example one learned by scriptural and historical study. Given this orientation, a mystical religion, which minimizes historical actualities and moral precept because it prefers a more abstract and general truth and vision *above* history, seems to be "impersonal."

The situation is similar for the American school of personal idealism represented first by Borden Parker Bowne and in the 1940s by Edgar Sheffield Brightman. To be a "person" means to be active in the use of reason and to be morally self-determining. It is precisely on this count, rational and ethical self-determination, that the otherworldliness and passivity of mysticism seem to make it "impersonal."[12]

In a third strand of Protestant theology, that of the neo-orthodoxy identified with Karl Barth, Emil Brunner, and others, the mystical and the personal are regarded as antithetical *types* of religion—the one of immanence, the other of transcendence. Christianity is described as a personal faith in which man is addressed by God in the revelatory word "thou." Mysticism is described as a type of religion in which the elements of the personal— addressability and response—are lacking and a pattern of "ascent" is preferred. Following this line of thinking, it becomes possible to say that mysticism is inherently an unchristian way of being religious. This is precisely what Emil Brunner, whose views of mysticism will occupy us later, does say.

No question is more important in the approach of the Christian thinker to mysticism than the question of the relationship between the mystical and the personal. Can the mystical and the personal coexist? Might they supplement and reinforce each other? Are they possibly antithetical? These are the questions that will occupy us in final chapters.

Mysticism and Tradition

Often the words "mystical" and "mysticism" simply convey the idea of being religious, and among those who are religious, the words are strongly approved. That the word "mystical" is used, quite simply, to mean "religious experience" is well illustrated in the following excerpt from a debate on the existence of God between Bertrand Russell and Father F. C. Copleston, the English Jesuit and historian of philosophy:

> **Copleston:** By religious experience I don't mean simply feeling good. I mean a loving, but unclear, awareness of some object which irresistibly seems to the experiencer as something transcending the self, something transcending all the normal objects of experience, something which cannot be pictured or conceptualized, but of the reality of which doubt is impossible—at least during the experience.
>
> **Russell:** If there's a crowd in a room and there's a clock in a room, they can all see the clock. The fact that they can all see it tends to make them think that it's not an hallucination: whereas these religious experiences do tend to be very private.
>
> **Copleston:** Yes, they do. I'm speaking strictly of mystical experience proper, and I certainly don't include, by the way, what are called visions. I mean simply the experience, and I quite admit it's indefinable, of the transcendent object or of what seems to be a transcendent object. I remember Julian Huxley in some

lecture saying that religious experience, or mystical experience, is as much a real experience as falling in love or appreciating poetry and art. Well, I believe that when we appreciate poetry and art we appreciate definite poems or a definite work of art. If we fall in love, well, we fall in love with somebody and not with nobody.[13]

This segment of the debate shows that while Father Copleston does not regard religious, or "mystical," experience as a "strict proof" of the existence of God, he does not believe that it can be explained in wholly subjective terms either. It is also clear that here he does not mean by mystical experience something that is accessible only to a visionary with special spiritual endowments. It is rather as if to be mystical were simply to be religious.

To many the word "mysticism" will thus suggest the idea of prayer, perhaps prayer at its best, and even a kind of expertise in prayer. The most eminent advocate of this traditional approach to the study of mysticism is Evelyn Underhill, whose scholarly works are, as Walter Kaufmann put it, more of a "tribute" to mysticism than an analysis of it. "In mysticism," Underhill says,

that love of truth which we saw as the beginning of all philosophy leaves the merely intellectual sphere, and takes on the assured aspect of a personal passion. Where the philosopher guesses and argues, the mystic lives and looks; and speaks, consequently, the disconcerting language of first-hand experience, not the neat dialectic of the schools. Hence whilst the Absolute of the metaphysicians remains a diagram—impersonal and unattainable—the Absolute of the mystics is lovable, attainable, alive.[14]

Of those who associate the word "mysticism" with prayer—approvingly—there are those who take, let us say, a democratic view. All may pray. All may, therefore, in a sense be "mystics." Ernst Troeltsch has found this democratic view to be one important feature in the type of mysticism expressed in the Protestant sectarian reformation as distinguished from medieval Catholic mysticism. While Catholic mysticism of the Middle Ages did encourage individualism, it was, according to Troeltsch, still under the protection of the church and under the discipline of religious orders and did not develop the full individualism of Protestant spirituality. "Protestant mysticism, on the contrary, learnt to regard itself as the outcome of the idea of the priesthood of all believers, and of the personal religion of conviction, and thus it was able to make an independent stand."[15] The Baptists, the Anabaptists, the Mennonites and Moravians, the Quakers, the Methodists, the American frontiersmen in their sawdust meeting houses—the whole sectarian reformation is informed by the kind of piety that suggests that in prayer all men are equals, that whatever is possible for some is possible for all.

But there have always been those who preferred to acknowledge an expertise in prayer, a cultivation of the art of prayer; and while this is a generally Catholic emphasis—exemplified above all in *The Spiritual Exercises* of St. Ignatius Loyola and in *The Life of St. Teresa*—it is not exclusively so. Writing in the sixties, Olive Wyon, the English translator of German theological books, said that "ignorance of the life of prayer is responsible for much of the 'arrested development' so common with the Church today. We tolerate haphazard method and carelessness in spiritual matters which we would not endure for a moment in the ordinary affairs of life and business."[16]

In this view, to pray is, among other things, to practice an art or to learn a method, in which some persons are bound to be more expert than others. One may be spiritually apt and "develop," or one may be a spiritual sluggard and suffer "arrested development." Perhaps this view should be called a non-Calvinist orientation, because in it there is lacking much of the sense of the impropriety of self-help and self-cultivation—the Calvinist fear that to make an effort on one's own part is to interfere with a humble reception of grace.[17]

Within the household of prayer, these two groups are likely to misunderstand each other. In the democratic view, the thought of a specialist in prayer goes against the grain. The privacy and isolation of experience called mystical seems to make it antithetical to the common man's experience. If mysticism is something that only a few special, cloistered people practice, then mysticism will seem to edge toward the freakish.

To the self-cultivators, the democrats of prayer seem without method, untaught by historical example. They mistake what is merely random for the free operation of the Holy Spirit, and they mistake what is merely widespread for what is normal and desirable.

This is the issue in a "traditional" concern for mysticism, a concern that largely equates mystical with religious experience and finds mysticism's value most of all in what it offers Christian devotion.

Mysticism as a Pattern

William James has said that if one were asked to characterize religion in the most general terms possible, it could be said to consist of "the belief that there is an unseen order, and that our supreme good lies in harmoniously adjusting ourselves thereto."[18]

These, of course, are very general terms indeed. If they are to be brought down to the concrete case, we will need to know what in a particular religion is meant by "unseen order" and what is meant by "harmoniously adjusting ourselves thereto." These are questions for the detailed work of the history of religions.

Just now, let us be content to think of "this world" as our workaday or commonsense world, in which plans are made and schedules are kept—the level of life on which we live most of the time and on which we care what time it is and what duties need to be discharged. This is the world of the calendar and of appointments—the life that deals with times and places. And since we are shortly to glance at samples of mysticism in various cultures, let us leave it open as to what meaning, precisely, will attach to "that world." For the Christian "that world" is God's world and to speak of an "adjustment" between these worlds is to speak somehow of the work of Christ. We can gain a glimpse into the meaning of "that world" by means of the sense of oppression and limitation that overcomes anyone who feels himself constricted by a calendar and schedule: In Frost's fine phrase, "I have promises to keep and miles to go before I sleep." Everyone champs at an exclusive confinement to places and times.

Yearning thus for the ideal can be escapism. Escapism is, in a way, the impotent witness to this yearning. We fix on this or that and hope it will draw us out of times and places and their confinement, the confinement of *chronos*. Perhaps a new job, a redecorated room, or a vacation is our prescription. The appetite of the consumer and the methods of the advertiser conspire to disguise our confinement to time and its consequent deadening effect. Then these escapist efforts, too, take their place in chronological time and themselves become confining. The new job becomes the old job; the new room becomes worn and familiar; the vacation becomes tiresome. Even prayer can be confining when it becomes a moment at some time on the clock instead of a moment of incandescence. Whatever is regularized loses its charm and therefore its power, and we always sense some insufficiency about mere efficiency. There must be some transcending of times and places, or at least we hope and yearn for experiences in which they are transcended. The problem is how to live in a world that needs to be regularized, and that is *necessarily* chronological, without stifling the transcendent; and how to celebrate the transcendent in a way that enhances and does not efface, regularity and chronology.

There is, then, a yearning for a world, a "that world," that does not annul time and space but transcends an *exclusive* preoccupation with them, invests them with meaning, and makes them less confining.

Various religions differ on the particular makeup of these worlds. A given religious culture has a structure of myths, symbols, practice, and theory composing its world view, which both shows and enacts the assumed relationship between "this world" and "that world." This structure both declares and celebrates moments of change in the relationship between these worlds. Is James's "unseen order," or "that world," to be identified with the God of theism? If so, to what extent does our "adjusting ourselves thereto" consist in a moral effort to conform to that which theists call God's will? To what extent are we to be concerned, in this moral effort, only with our individual lives, our individual, private moral efforts? Or are we to achieve this adjustment by, say, political involvement, exhortation, or social and ethical exertion? To what extent are we to "achieve" it at all? Is it rather to be bestowed by a soteriological figure? Or, to speak of other cultures, is "this world" an appearance and "that world" its deep, underlying meaning that is, Tao or Brahma? Is the relationship between the two worlds a matter of unveiling the one and revealing the other, which has lain there all the time unnoticed?

Questions like these concern the details of the world view of particular religious cultures. Bypassing the question of the contents, what concerns us here is simply the *relationship* between these two worlds, because mysticism is better understood as a type of relationship between these worlds than exclusively in terms of their content.[19]

If it is appropriate to say of mysticism that, at a reflective distance, it "takes" or "has" a world view, that view is the assumption of a world of appearance (this world) and a world of reality (that world), which the world of appearance implies and dimly manifests. The problem of religion, its task and its program, is the relationship between these two worlds. The *epistemological* aim of mysticism is thus to know "that world" at first hand and not by inference. The *ethical* aim is likewise an immediacy—to be so thoroughly united with the God of "that world" that no moral effort need be expended nor moral judgment exercised.

But wait. There is something anomalous about saying that mysticism's "aim" is immediacy. If one has an aim, then one does not yet have that at which one aims. And if the aim is immediacy, how can aiming help to achieve it. This anomaly is an inherent characteristic of mysticism and partly accounts for its complex character. Mysticism does not, as is sometimes and perhaps erroneously said of innocent primitive religious life, *begin* with immediacy. It begins with a separation between the two worlds, and it seeks to bind them together again. Mysticism is thus to be distinguished from a simple primitive innocence that sees no separation.[20] Mysticism appears to be not innocence itself but a conscious, effortful imitation of innocence.

The mystic's relationship to his aim, his object, or his God is not that of an infant's symbiotic relationship with his mother. His relationship is that of the adolescent who knows and feels a separation between himself and some center of meaning, some mother principle. The mystic is initially faced with a distance that must be overcome and an object or a state of being that is not simply given but must be won. When it is won, his relationship with his desired object or state is that of identity, or at least very close to identity. In Baron von Hügel's words, "It is as though the initial excess of distance avenged itself, at the end in an excess of closeness."[21]

Mysticism, thus, involves *an immediacy that is by some means recovered or achieved*. It must therefore be understood in two aspects.

Preliminarily, mysticism can involve the *practical* question of how to achieve a desired object or state—how to use "this world" in such a way as to join it with "that world." To say that this preliminary stage is "practical" does not imply that it is practical in the sense of having a program of social action and reform. It is a stage not primarily concerned with remaking "this world" in accordance with a vision of "that world."[22] The practicality of this stage does not mean that the mystic focuses on "this world" as an end. He pays attention to "this world" only insofar as he can make use of it to attain his ultimate aim, "that world."

At this preliminary stage, with respect both to ethics and epistemology, there is lacking the passivity that exists ultimately in mysticism. The preparatory stage, in fact, can involve a rigorous moral activism. While this preparation may with some justification be regarded as an ascetic "withdrawal," there is no denying the fact that asceticism involves a rigorous self-assertion in order to achieve self-denial. This preliminary stage is also characterized by an intellectual activism that historically has taken the forms either of analytical thinking or mystical lyricism. The rational discursus of medieval scholasticism is an example of the former; the devotions of St. Francis, an example of the latter. What needs to be emphasized is that in the preliminary stage of preparation, as opposed to the ultimate stage of union, mysticism is not inconsistent with epistemological and ethical activism. The mystic actively seeks to know and actively seeks to do good.

Ultimately, however, mysticism involves an immediacy for which words of description, rational analysis, and moral injunctions are inadequate. The techniques of "this world" only serve for an arm's length view of "that world." They do not give us an immediate union with it. Ineffability, moral indifferentism, and passivism are thus necessary features of mysticism in its ultimate phase. Ultimately, the mystic is typically unable to speak of the end he has achieved because he feels himself to be united with this end, and any description of an object presumes a distance between the object and himself. His experience of union with his object seems to annul this presumed distance. To speak at all of this object while in this ultimate state would reinstate the distance between himself and his object and place him on a less than ultimate rung of the ladder of ascent. The mystic, thus, ultimately has no words of description; he is at one with what he seeks.

Moreover, ultimately, the rigorous moral effort, the asceticism that is typical of the preliminary stage of preparation, has no place, since the mystic's objective has been achieved. In fact, to expend any moral effort is evidence that the end has not yet been achieved, that there is still a distance to be traveled. In the ultimate state of union with his object the mystic makes no moral choices. He is presumed to be at one with goodness itself. Since he has achieved his ethical goal, he is now entirely passive; for to be active is evidence that the goal has yet to be achieved. He is now entirely "indifferent" (i.e., he does not concern himself with moral differences) to various, relative goods, since he has achieved and is supposedly united with the absolute good.

In viewing mysticism as a pattern with a preliminary and ultimate stage, we find that contrary things can be true of mysticism as a whole. In ethics it can be both passive and active; in reason, both silent and analytical; and in all, paradoxical. This double aspect of mysticism involves it in three besetting philosophical issues:

First, what is the nature of the knowledge the mystic claims to have? How does the mystic's claim to immediate knowledge of "that world" relate to all men's common knowledge of "this world"? Can there be a "reason above reason" without annihilating reason altogether? This is the issue that is indicated when it is said that mysticism is irrational. In the mystic's ultimate stage of union, he appears to abandon the commonsense world altogether. Yet in the preliminary stage of preparation, he pays close attention to it.

Second, what is the nature of the moral life that mysticism implies? How are this-worldly action, effort, and decision related to that-worldly contemplation and passivity? Are contemplation and social service antithetical?

Third, what is mysticism's estimate of man? Is man

properly engaged in this-worldly rational and ethical interests? Or is his nature essentially divine and better left untouched by the things of this world? One great philosophical value of a study of mysticism is that it makes these perennial questions particularly acute.

Mysticism is thus difficult to define not only because of its long history and cultural variety but because it envisions not a single world view but a two-stage program for uniting "this world" and "that world."

PART TWO
Sources

If there should rise
Suddenly within the skies
Sunburst of a thousand suns
Flooding earth with rays undreamed-of,
Then might be that Holy One's
Majesty and glory dreamed of!
                    —The Bhagavad-Gita 11. 12

As water penetrates and is drunk in by the sponge, so it
seemed to me, did the Divinity fill my soul. . . . And I heard
him say also: "Labor thou not to hold Me within thyself
enclosed, but enclose thou thyself within Me."
                    —St. Teresa, *Relations* III

Chapter 2
Soundings in Eastern Mysticism

Every mystic assumes a world of appearance, a *this world*, and a world of deeper reality, a *that world*, which this workaday world can dimly manifest—provided it is viewed rightly. How then is the mystic to look at "this world" so that he will come to know "that world"? This is the question that lies behind every mystic's program: How can I know the real, obscured as it is by the everyday appearance?

Hinduism

Once a man woke up in the middle of the night because he wished to smoke, but then he thought he would have to go to his neighbor's to get a light in order to smoke, and so he walked to his neighbor's house and knocked on the door. "The man said: 'I wish to smoke. Can you give me a light?' The neighbor replied: 'Bah! What is the matter with you? You have taken so much trouble to come and [awaken] us at this hour, when in your hand, you have a lighted lantern!'" This is a story told by the nineteenth-century Hindu Ramakrishna, who adds a moral that could be taken as the slogan of Hindu mysticism: "What a man wants is already within him; but he still wanders here and there in search of it."[1] When you seek that which is transcendent, look to

immanence, look within yourself. You will find that it is
only a false distinction between the two that occasions
your search. And so—be still. That which you seek, you
already have, you already are; but you must, by some
means, *discover* that this is so.

The doctrine of the basic identity of the self and the
reality that the self seeks—the identity of Atman and
Brahman—is the essence of Hindu monism stated as a
doctrine of the school of Advaita Vedanta. It is one of the
most interesting philosophies for the study of speculative, which is to say philosophical, mysticism because,
from the Westerner's individualistic perspective, it not
only allows but encourages mystical "absorption" of the
self. It is, however, only one of many possible
philosophies within India's immensely long and varied
religious history.[2] In the nineteenth century, when
Westerners like Schopenhauer, Emerson, and Thoreau
began to look appreciatively at such "Hindoo" doctrines
as happened to come their way through German and
English translators, this Atman-Brahman doctrine
seemed almost the whole of Eastern wisdom. Wasn't it
transcendentalism? And, even better, exotic? Today,
with the variety of sources available to the historian of
religion, no one should assume that Hinduism is easily
summarized with a slogan. Nor do we find the essence of
mysticism by simply looking eastward. In fact, much of
Hindu wisdom is addressed to the practical everyday
world of the here and now.[3]

Another and equally interesting Hindu view, or rather
practice, is *Bhakti,* the way of devotion. It suggests an
idea of the deity-devotee relationship that is quite
different from identification or absorption. In Bhakti the
worshiper retains his individuality; the divine object is
personified; and the language that proceeds between the
two is lyrical, emotional, and personal. Confining our
attention in this section to Hindu monism and to the
more dualistic and personalistic Bhakti, we need to
consider how or whether these different approaches

could be types of mysticism. Are they the "recovery of immediacy" and if so, in what sense?

First, let us sketch some of the background, focusing on three phases—the infancy of primitive Hinduism and its nature worship, the adolescence of philosophical reflection, and the return home of Bhakti worship with its recovery, on an entirely new level, of primitive personalism.

Primitive Hinduism. Excavations made at Mohenjo-daro and Harappa, which are names of ancient cities in what is now West Pakistan, give us some access to the religious life of a pre-Vedic civilization of the Indus Valley that existed about 2500 B.C. or contemporaneously with ancient Egypt and Babylon. Evidence points to the worship of nature spirits, phallic rites, and cults of mother goddesses, as well as to representations of seated, meditating figures. Around 1500 B.C. this original civilization was overtaken by a fair-skinned people who called themselves Aryans ("noblemen") and drove the dark-skinned Dravidians southward. It is probable that something of this conflict is reflected in the important Hindu epic *Mahabharata,* of which the classic Bhagavad-Gita is the most famous part.

The Aryan invasion marks the beginning of the period of the Vedas, or "Books of Knowledge," which are the most authoritative scripture (sruti) of Hinduism and which reflect the period from about 1500 to 1000 B.C. The Vedas are comprised of prayers and praises addressed to a great number of nature gods. Indra (thunder and storm, or power), Varuna (righteousness), Agni (fire sacrifice), Vayu (wind), Soma (sacred drink), and others. The chief motifs are polytheism and nature worship: "Varuna poured out the leather-bag, opening downward, upon the heaven and the earth and mid-region. Thereby does the lord of the whole creation moisten thoroughly the expanse of earth, as rain does the corn."[4]

Since Agni, the god of fire, was important to the sacrifice, he gained some prominence as a god who mediates between the other gods and man:

May Agni, the chief priest, who possesses the insight of a
sage, who is truthful, widely renown, and divine, come
here with the gods.

O Agni, be easy of access to us as a father to his son. Join
us for our well being.[5]

The period of the *Brahmanas* (or "sacrificial manuals,"
ca. 1000–500 B.C.) was characterized by an even further
emphasis on the importance of the sacrifice. Salvation
depended on a sacrifice perfectly performed and, therefore, upon the Brahman priests who knew how to
perform it. This reflective interest in sacrifices marks a
transition from primitivism to metaphysical speculation
because the sacrifices came to be regarded not as
appeasements to the gods but, if properly performed, as
more powerful than the gods themselves. They were not
the "ordinary magic of spells and incantations, but the
repository of the cosmic secrets and cosmic forces."[6] The
slightest inaccuracy in the prayer or sacrifice could ruin
everything—even for the gods. Tvashtar, it is told, had
performed a sacrifice for the birth of a son who might kill
Indra, but due to a mispronunciation the son was killed
by Indra. The sacrifices give access to a deeper meaning,
deeper and more powerful than the gods. It takes but a
small adjustment to consider that it is by means of
reflection rather than sacrifice that one attains access to
the deeper meaning.

Philosophical Hinduism. The second period (*ca.*
800–600 B.C.) is that of philosophical Hinduism, the
period of the *Upanishads,* a term which means "sitting
near a teacher." The overwhelming importance in
Brahmanism of ritual and sacrifice could allow attention
to center on the possibility of some single principle or law
in terms of which the sacrifice could be efficacious. The
individual identities of the gods now became obscured,
and it was possible to see them as representatives of a
deeper, single principle. Not all Hindu reflection was
thus led toward a single underlying principle, however.

Of the six classic schools, some were monistic, some pluralistic, and some dualistic. But in the movement from polytheistic nature worship to monism, all deities, in fact all things, were seen as manifestations of the one reality, Brahman.

The teaching of the Upanishads, since they came at the end of the Vedas, is called Vedanta, *anta* meaning "end." In Advaita (nondualistic) Vedanta the aim of man is to realize the essential unity of all things and the identity of his inmost self, Atman, with this deepest reality, Brahman. This identity is the true state of affairs, although this truth is obscured by the inscrutibility of divine creativity (maya). To see things as they really are, one must be instructed and attain knowledge (jnana). A man's salvation is thus seen to lie in his ability to "see" into reality, and he may be helped to do so by some ascetic practice or yoga. Apart from such a realization, he is doomed in future lives to transmigrate from one body to another in an endless cycle (samsara) in which, according to the law of Karma, he can improve or worsen his status depending on his behavior in various lives. In the Chandogya Upanishad, we find Aruni instructing his son, Shvetaketu, in the monistic doctrine:

> Just as, my dear, through the comprehension of one lump of clay all that is made of clay would become comprehended—for the modification is occasioned only on account of a convention of speech, it is only a name; while clay as such alone is the reality. Just as, my dear, through the comprehension of one ingot of iron all that is made of iron would become comprehended—for the modification is occasioned only on account of a convention of speech, it is only a name; while iron as such alone is the reality. . . . So, my dear, is that instruction.[7]

The view here is that the essence of clay objects lies in the clay. *What* the thing is is not a clay pitcher or plate but *really* just clay. Similarly, a man's essence lies not in that which differentiates him as a certain *kind* of being, such as Aristotle's "de-finition" of man as a rational animal. His essence is simply undifferentiated being itself. All kinds of things are *really* one thing. To remove the illusion of man's distinctiveness is to achieve the wisdom and oneness of Brahman and Atman. This is the purpose of Aruni's instruction to his son, Shvetaketu.

> "Bring hither a fig from there." "Here it is, sir." "Break it." "It is broken, sir." "What do you see there?" "These extremely fine seeds, sir." "Of these, please break one." "It is broken, sir." "What do you see there?" "Nothing at all, sir." Then he said to Shvetaketu: "Verily, my dear, that subtle essence which you do not perceive—from that very essence, indeed, my dear, does this great fig tree thus arise. Believe me, my dear, that which is the subtle essence—this whole world has that essence for its Self; that is the Real [satya, truth]; that is the Self; that [subtle essence] art thou, Shvetaketu."[8]

Shankara (*ca*. A.D. 800) founder of the school of Advaita Vedantic philosophy developed this formula *tat-tvam asi* ("that art thou") into a systematic doctrine of the identity of the self with Brahman. His thought lays great stress on the unreliability of man's sense experience for discerning the true nature of things. We are entrapped by ignorance (*avidya*—"nonknowledge") if we think sensed objects are real. We are tempted to regard them as real by the active, creative power that is at work in the world—maya. We are mistaken when we think of the phenomenal world as ultimately real, just as we are mistaken when we see a rope lying in the road at twilight and think, "There is a snake." The enlightened man is one who clears his distorted vision and sees that it is not sensed objects that are real but Brahman.

The paradox of mysticism is that it must teach what cannot be taught—that that which one seeks is, in reality, already attained. The paradox is evident in the slogan "He who realizes Brahman through knowing becomes Brahman." The basic paradox, according to Heinrich Zimmer, "is that, though the identity of jiva [the self] and Brahman, which is the sole permanent reality, is beyond change, nevertheless it must be realized and reestablished by means of a laborious process of temporal human endeavor. The case is compared to that of a man who has forgotten the precious jewel he wears about his neck and so suffers grief and anxiety, believing it to be lost. When he meets someone who points it out to him, nothing is changed except his ignorance—but this (at least to him) means a great deal."[9]

Devotional Hinduism: Bhakti. With Shankara and Advaita Vedanta, Hindu mysticism reached a highly abstract expression. An ascetic and intellectual frame of mind leaves out much in human nature that requires expression as well—a heart filled with devotion for a personal God rather than a mind reflecting coldly on an abstract principle. Moreover, there is no doubt that a preoccupation with knowledge as a means of salvation quite simply ignores the salvation of the ignorant and those of lower caste. In response to such needs, around the first century A.D. there developed a renewal of a devotional emphasis in religious practice that no doubt had been a force within Hinduism since ancient times. This is the movement called Bhakti, or devotional religion, which is preeminently represented in literary form in the Bhagavad-Gita.

In Bhakti, there are several new emphases and implied criticisms of other ways:

1. The religious ritual is quite simple and accessible to the individual worshiper who might offer his god a bit of oil or milk, a scrap of bright cloth, or a flower at a simple home shrine. Worship is not dependent on the expertise of the Brahman priests.

> Whatever man gives me
> In true devotion:
> Fruit or water,
> A leaf, a flower:
> I will accept it.
> That gift is love,
> His heart's dedication.[10]

2. The object of such devotion is a theistic (i.e., a particular and personal) god. There is interest in the god's heroic deeds, loves, and victories—all of which are real enough to be vividly imagined. Here is a god who is like ourselves yet able to perform acts of redemption:

> Give me your whole heart,
> Love and adore me,
> Worship me always,
> Bow to me only,
> And you shall find me:
> This is my promise
> Who love you dearly.
>
> Lay down all duties
> In me, your refuge.
> Fear no longer,
> For I will save you
> From sin and from bondage.[11]

3. The metaphysical assumptions in Bhakti, as they are represented in the Bhagavad-Gita, are more dualistic than the monistic Vedantism that we have been focusing on. In the Gita, the dualistic Sankyan philosophical outlook points to two realities: purusha (soul) and prakriti (matter). Prakriti expresses itself in three *gunas,* which combine in various proportions to make up the world and every sort of thing in it.[12] The devotee must be able to "discriminate" between the two realities of soul and matter. Then he can freely participate in action, but with a special attitude, that is, "free from all attachments to the results" of the action.

What is there of mysticism in the two aspects of Hinduism—monistic Vedantism and Bhakti? Mysticism as the "recovery of immediacy" assumes a two-layer world—a "this world" and a "that world," and it is bent on reuniting these two worlds. It cannot be said that the primitive stage of Hinduism is representative of mysticism in this sense, because the so-called primitive mind does not engage in reflective thought about the division between these two worlds. If there were such a thing as a purely primitive "type," and this is entirely open to question, it would consist of life lived in a spirit-filled world of unreflective immediacy. For the primitive, the two worlds are, really, only one world. The primitive *begins* with a state of affairs with which the mystic—at a stage of more advanced reflection—does not *begin* but seeks to be reunited. The mystic seeks that immediacy which the primitive already possesses. Just as an infant existing in symbiotic love does not seek love with adolescent yearning, the primitive does not seek to recover immediacy since he has not yet lost it.

In the monistic Vedantism to which it is possible to point in certain Upanishads, there arrives a full-fledged mysticism of the speculative type: an apprentice is taught by a master to discern the distinction between "this world" and "that world," then is taught that on a deeper level of philosophical reflection the two worlds are really one. Here, the means for bridging the gap is *knowledge.* This type of speculative mysticism has its counterpart in the philosopher-mystics of the West—in Meister Eckhart, Pseudo-Dionysius, and Plotinus, who set the pattern for Western mysticism.

Devotional mysticism, or as it is usual to say in the West, "practical" mysticism, or pietism, is an attempt to bridge the gap between the two worlds, not through the use of *thought* alone but through feelings and actions coupled with thought. What I do—a practical act of worship—will reunite me with the god to whom I am devoted. In Bhakti we have something of the same practical devotional spirit that exists in St. Francis of Assisi or St. Teresa of Avila—a reunion achieved by the practical means of devotion. In a way, it is a return to an original, unreflective, primitive innocence; but, inasmuch as it is a "return," it is not the same as primitive innocence. The man who becomes childlike is not thereby simply a child.

Bhakti, and devotional mysticism generally, present some difficulty with respect to matching them to the definition of mysticism as "an immediacy that is recovered." But if we have an appreciation for the various

meanings of immediacy (see pp. 186-97), it is easier to
see in what sense Bhakti and the practical mysticism or
pietism of the West could be termed mystical and in what
sense they could not. Of the three metaphors of
immediacy (spatial—immediacy of merging; temporal—
immediacy of the "now"; and spontaneity, which denies
an intervening means), Bhakti is the recovery of
immediacy in the last sense, of denying an intervening
means between the worshiper and his deity. Bhakti is
clearly not the recovery of immediacy in the first sense of
immediacy, which denies a separation of two identities.
But as a form of worship it is "immediate." It requires
only sincerity of the heart. The worshiper does not first
need to engage the services of the Brahman priests to
perform the sacrifice. The mediating function of the
religious expert, the priest, is minimized. Nothing
intervenes between the self and its god. In this sense
immediacy is a keynote in devotional religion. But it is
not an immediacy of *merging* or an identity of the devotee
and his god. The personhood of the devotee remains
intact. He is not absorbed by an impersonal divine
substance. A song by Tukaram makes the point admira-
bly:

> Can water quaff itself?
> Can trees taste of the fruit they bear?
> He who worships God must stand distinct from Him,
> So only shall he know the joyful love of God;
> For if he say that God and he are one,
> That joy, that love, shall vanish instantly away.
>
> Pray no more for utter oneness with God:
> Where were the beauty if jewel and setting were one?
> The heat and the shade are two,
> If not, where were the comfort of shade?
> Mother and child are two,
> If not, where were love?
> When after long being sundered, they meet
> What joy do they feel, the mother and child!
> Where were joy, if the two were one?
> Pray, then, no more for utter oneness with God.[13]

In speculative mysticism the attention is directed toward an impersonal object: "Being" or the "One" or the "Godhead." In devotional mysticism the object is more personal. The question is that if speculative mysticism is mysticism, is it possible to say that the devotional type is mysticism as well? Do they have anything in common? We can suggest that both have in common a nonmanagerial relationship with what is worshiped. The priest, with his sacrificial equipment and knowledge, is a manager, not a devotee. He deals with the "Holy" by means of the particular technology of his profession. The speculative mystic addresses himself to an impersonal "Something"; he does so, however, as one who "beholds" it, not as one who copes with it in a managerial way. The devotional or practical mystic addresses himself not to a Something but to a Someone; but the practical mystic, too, rather than being manipulative, presents himself and his heart in a prayer of devotion.

Buddhism

Buddhism was originally a movement that offered a "middle way" between the extremes of asceticism and worldly desire. It is told that a monk named Sona, who was given to excessive discipline, had paced up and down until his feet bled—in the vain attempt to achieve the right concentration of mind. His failure in the face of such austerities brought him to the point of despair, and the Buddha offered him counsel:

"Now, Sona, were you not a clever musician and skilled lute player formerly, when you were a layman?"

"Yes, Sir."

"Now what do you think when the strings of your lute become too tight, could you get the right tune, or was it then fit to play?"

"No indeed, Sir."

"Likewise, when the lute strings become too slack, could you get the right tune or was it then fit to play?"

"No indeed, Sir."

"But when the lute strings were neither too tight nor too slack but were keyed to an even pitch then did it give the right tune?"

"Yes indeed, Sir."

"Even so, Sona, too much zeal conduces to restlessness and too much slackness conduces to mental sloth."[14]

The Buddha had earlier tried just such austerities; he had fasted, as it is said, until his spine touched his stomach. Such efforts he found futile, and in his moment of enlightenment he found a "middle way."

The Buddha (which title simply means "the awakened one") is Siddhartha Gautama—to give his first and last names. He is also called Sakyamuni, or the silent sage of the Sakya people (his native clansmen), as well as Tathagata, the one who has gone "thus" along the right path. He was born a prince about the sixth century B.C. near Nepal, and tradition pictures his early life as luxurious and soft.

> I was tenderly cared for, monks, supremely so, infinitely so. At my father's home lotus pools were made for me—in one place for the blue lotus flowers, in one place for white lotus flowers, and in one place for red lotus flowers—blossoming for my sake. And, monks, I used only unguents from Benares. Of Benares fabric were my three robes. Day and night a white umbrella was held over me, so that I might not be troubled by cold, heat, dust, chaff or dew. I dwelt in three palaces, monks: in one for the cold, in one for the summer, and in one for the rainy season.[15]

At about age thirty he left his wife and son to take up a life of spiritual discipline. While meditating under a fig tree, since then called the tree of enlightenment, "bodhi" or "bo" tree, he found enlightenment and passed the next forty years as a wandering teacher who organized his disciples into communities of monks. He seems to have been a teacher who did not make divine claims for himself but was venerated as one who indicated the divine path for others. When people asked the Buddha what kind of being he was, he identified himself by reference to his experience. "Are you a god?" "No." "An angel?" "No." "A saint?" "No." "Then what are you?" The Buddha replied, "I am awake."[16] The "three jewels" of Buddhism are the Buddha; the Dharma, or his teaching; and the Sangha, or order of monks. These are to Buddhists of all schools the holiest things, and meditating on them is the "threefold refuge."

In the deer park at Benares, the Buddha proclaimed his teaching (Dharma)—the Four Noble Truths and the Noble Eightfold Path. These are much easier to list than to understand.[17]

The Four Noble Truths

1. The truth of suffering (dukkha). All the "aggregates" of existence are transient, are subject to suffering, and are anatta (without a permanent soul).
2. The origin of suffering is desire (tanha) or a clinging to one's ego as separate.
3. The extinction of suffering consists in the extinction of desire.
4. The path that leads to the extinction of suffering is the Noble Eightfold Path, or the Middle Way.

The Noble Eightfold Path

1. *Right Understanding.* Having knowledge of the doctrine. Understanding that existence is impermanent. Understanding the Four Noble Truths, Karma, and the chain of dependent origination.
2. *Right-Mindedness.* Renunciation of the worldly life and all obstacles that stand in the way of the realization of one's ideals. A right aspiration. Coming to know what one really wants.

The above virtues comprise the "higher wisdom," which can be understood as a beginning level and also, paradoxically, as an outcome or final stage of the path.

3. *Right Speech.* Refraining from lying, gossip, or harsh or tactless speech.
4. *Right Action.* Refraining from murder, stealing, and sexual misconduct.
5. *Right Livelihood.* Refraining from ignoble occupations such as trading in arms, intoxicants, poisons, or prostitution.

These three virtues comprise the "ethical disciplines" and are not only guides for good conduct but preparations for further stages of meditation and the attainment of the higher wisdom.

6. *Right Effort.* The right effort of the will to eliminate evil thoughts that have arisen or might arise and the effort to encourage good thoughts.
7. *Right Mindfulness.* Keeping the proper vigilance over one's internal state. Mindfulness of the body, its postures, attitudes, and breathing. Mindfulness of feelings with a view to maintaining equilibrium between pleasant and unpleasant feelings. Mindfulness of states of mind (love, hate, joy, hope, fear) so that one is not carried away by a mood of anger.
8. *Right Concentration.* The practitioner sets himself to transcending normal, discursive understanding and to reaching a state of samadhi, or trance.

These last three elements comprise the "mental discipline" that closely resembles the techniques of the raja-yoga of Patanjali.[18]

In assessing the Buddha's religion with respect to mysticism, we need to consider that the aim of the Buddha's path is not an intellectual understanding of doctrines. It is not a philosophy to be adopted but a technique to be attempted. The aim is practical. Man's general situation in life is compared to the specific one of a man who has been wounded by an arrow. What the man needs most is to have the arrow withdrawn to alleviate his suffering. To give priority to metaphysical questions would be as irrelevant to man's actual situation as to ask the nature of the bow and to inquire of the eye and hair color of the archer. Though the case is different with the later Mahayana Buddhism, the Buddha's own religion is not a mysticism of the speculative type, for it does not interest itself in the nature of a divine being. The fact is, there are some grounds for dissociating Buddhism and mysticism.

Buddhism understands the self as a temporary assemblage of "aggregates." There is no permanent or immortal "soul," or Atman. Man's existence is anatta, or without soul. A man's nails teeth, skin, and other bodily parts—as well as his sensations, perception, and consciousness—are only temporarily located in a spot which we, for convenience, designate by his name. In a famous analogy, man is compared to a chariot, a conglomerate of "axle, wheels, frame, reins, yoke, spokes, etc."[19] If the components of the chariot were taken apart, the chariot itself would cease to exist. Such a view runs counter to a usual outlook of mysticism, which finds in man a soul, or its counterpart, that when stripped of its illusory encasement is identical with a higher reality. As Monistic Hinduism expresses it, Atman and Brahman are "really" the same. While the program that Buddhism directs is indeed a stripping away of illusion (maya), the end in view is simply Nirvana or the snuffing out of existence (i.e., suffering), just as the flame of a candle is snuffed out. Buddhism is, therefore, sometimes called an atheistic religion, because it envisions no higher reality as man's end. The goal is quite simply nothingness, Nirvana.

The question is whether a religion which thus lacks a transcendent being can be designated "mystical." On this and similar grounds, some writers in fact deny that Theravada Buddhism is a type of mysticism.[20] When we think of the practical aspects of Buddhism, however, we find that like many forms of mysticism, it is a teaching that lends itself to being outlined in progressive stages. It is true that Buddhism is less hierarchical than Christian mysticism and that the end is not "union" with a "higher" reality but simply the cessation of illusory existence itself. But while Buddhism denies, in theory, the permanence of the soul, in practice it assumes a transmigration of the immaterial constituents of the self and makes room, in Hindu fashion, for a cycle of births governed by Karma. As with many forms of mystical instruction, one needs to be taught "the way," and it is outlined for the initiate in stages, beginning with the ethical discipline, which is more elementary, and ending with the more abstract mental disciplines, which are more advanced. With Buddhism, in contrast to Christian mysticism, it seems less appropriate to speak of the series as an "ascent" from lower to higher, but the end is certainly a mystical liberation and an awakening as to what is true about the nature of existence: it is nothing.

At first the Buddha's followers were simply "followers"; that is, they wandered with him here and there as mendicants. Eventually they became more institutionalized, and they retreated, during the rainy season, into places of shelter that became permanent monasteries. The Sangha, or religious community, thus became one of the three jewels of Buddhism. This earlier, monastic Buddhism is called Theravada (the sect of the Elders) or Hinayana (Buddhism of the lesser vehicle). Its ethical and religious ideal is the *Arhat*, the perfectly disciplined disciple—an ideal achieved not by a divine bestowal of grace but by a strict adherence to the Buddha's teaching. The Theravada's scripture is written in Pali, and in it the Buddha is a saint and moral example.

When we consider Mahayana Buddhism, we need to alter the picture of Buddhism as a practical, self-help technique. What must now be included is the reality of an "above" and a "beyond," as well as the reality of the bestowal of grace from the realm above. Mahayana

Buddhism (Buddhism of the greater vehicle), in contrast to Theravada, has as its chief feature the Bodhisattva, an enlightened, magnanimous person who has brought himself to the point of Nirvana and, in an act of compassion for those who have not advanced so far, returns to point the way to others. In later development, the Bodhisattva became a celestial being who was for all practical purposes indistinguishable from a god. The Mahayana literature, strongly reflects otherworldliness and a divine bestowal of grace. Prayers of the Pure Land school addressed to the heavenly Buddha, *Amitabha,* and to his realm of paradise, especially emphasize these themes:

> What words can picture the beauty and breadth
> Of that pure and glistening land?
> That land where the blossoms ne're wither from age,
> Where the golden gates gleam like purest water—
> The land that rises in terrace on terrace
> Of diamond-clad steps and shining jade—
> That land where there are none but fragrant bowers,
> Where the Utpala lotus unfolds itself freely.
> O hear the sweet tones from hillside and grove
> The All-Father's praise from the throats of the birds! . . .
>
> There ne'er was a country so brightened with gladness
> As the Land of the Pure there far off to the West.
> There stands Amitabha with shining adornments,
> He makes all things ready for the Eternal Feast.
> He draws every burdened soul up from the depths
> And lifts them up into his peaceful abode.
> The great transformation is accomplished for the worm
> Who is freed from the body's oppressive sorrows.
> It receives as a gift a spiritual body,
> A body which shines in the sea of spirits. [21]

The focus in Mahayana Buddhism is on the Buddha not so much as an historical personage as a celestial being or even a divine stuff or "Buddha essence." And, eventually, partly in alignment with Vedantism, there is the idea of a Buddha Essence (cf. Brahman), having many manifestations in innumerable earthly and heavenly Buddhas. It is also the idea of salvation and of help for man from divine beings that distinguishes Mahayana from Theravada Buddhism. If the distinction between a "this world" and a "that world" is the special hallmark of mysticism, then Mahayana Buddhism certainly invites the spirit of mysticism.

Taoism and Zen Buddhism

A bright little girl went home from the first day of school. In a dejected manner she confessed that she did not "even know how to turn the pages," a puzzling announcement since before going to school she had turned through many books, looking at each page and reading a few words. Perhaps too much teacher's first-day advice made something easy and natural seem difficult and complicated.

> A centipede was happy, quite,
> Until a frog in fun
> Said, "Pray, which leg comes after which?"
> This raised her mind to such a pitch,
> She lay distracted in a ditch
> Considering how to run.

> Anonymous, "The Puzzled Centipede"

Too much effort sometimes binds the gears. That is how we, in our motorized age, would express it. The ancient Chinese-Taoist philosophy was not concerned with mechanics but with an aesthetic apprehension of nature and nature's deeper underlying meaning. "The highest good is like that of water. The goodness of water is that it benefits the ten thousand creatures; yet itself does not scramble, but is content with the place that all men disdain."[22]

Quietism and love of paradox are themes charmingly represented in the Taoist classic the Tao-Te Ching, or "the Classic of the Way and Its Power," which according to tradition is the first philosophical work in Chinese history. It is ascribed to the shadowy, perhaps fictional character Lao-Tze, whose teachings, along with those of his disciple, Chuang-Tze, are called Taoism. According to tradition, Lao-Tze was born in 604 B.C. and was a contemporary of Confucius, with whom he often had disputes. The conflict between them, as we would put it today, was like that of a middle class, self-assertive, highly moral man taking issue with the views of an artistic, sensitive dropout who believes he sees something deeper to religious life than mere moralism. The Confucian type was the gentleman-scholar, the good, family man, the responsible citizen. The Taoist type was such a gentleman "seeking surcease from the cares of official life, . . . intoxicated by the beauties of nature or of the spirit."[23] The Confucians were moralists, but to the Taoists such moralizing and intellectualizing was a distortion of that deep reality hidden in nature and accessible only to an effortless acceptance of the Tao, or Way. This they tell us is best described as something natural, as "water" or as an "uncarved block."

Anyone who has ever experienced the failure of words to convey an experience that goes *beyond* words, will have some sympathy for the Taoist frame of mind. As against the Confucians, who put their reliance in the fitness of words to reflect a natural order and who called for a "rectification of names," the Taoists expressed in poetic form and parable the inadequacy of words to convey the Tao—a reality that goes beyond verbal distinctions.

> The Tao (Way) that can be told of
> Is not the eternal Tao;
> The name that can be named
> Is not the eternal name.[24]

Wisdom, the wisdom of this world, is of no use.

> Banish sageliness, discard wisdom,
> And the people will be benefited a hundredfold.
> Banish humanity, discard righteousness,

And the people will return to filial piety and
paternal affection.[25]

Intellectual efforts will not prevail to unite "this world"
and "that world" because when one comes to an
effortless realization of the way things are, he will see
that they are already unified. It is quite useless to be
worked up about some intellectual distinction between
things when, in deeper reality, there is no distinction.
Such useless fretting Taoism calls "three in the morning." "What is meant by 'three in the morning'? Well, a
keeper of monkeys once announced . . . that each was to
receive three [acorns] in the morning and four in the
evening. At this the monkeys were very angry. So the
keeper said that they might receive four in the morning
but three in the evening. With this all the monkeys were
pleased. Neither name nor reality were affected either
way, and yet the monkeys were pleased at the one and
angry at the other. This is also due to their ignorance
about the agreement of things. Therefore, the sages
harmonize the right and the wrong, and rest in nature
the equalizer."[26]

Thoughts from which all boundaries are loosened;
thoughts that begin "in the Secret Darkness;" "thoughts
that go back to a time when all was one—how can you
hope to reach them by the striving of a petty intelligence
or to ransack them by the light of your feeble sophistries?
You might as well look at Heaven through a reed or
measure earth with the point of a gimlet. Your instru-
ments are too small."[27]

"The mystic is silent not because he does not know,
but because he cannot explain," said William Ernest
Hocking. It is typical of mysticism to find that words
drawn from "this world" are inappropriate for expressing
the truth of "that world." "That world" is represented in
Taoism as the Tao, or Way, and it cannot be attained
either by an intellectual or moral effort—the chief bone
of contention with Confucians.

The inappropriateness of "this world's" goodness and

moral effort to the true effortless goodness of "that world" is illustrated in the following opinions of Lao-Tze, recorded in the extracts of Chuang Tze. Lao-Tze is depicted as in disagreement with Confucius, who has been moralizing on the necessity of duty:

> "Hum, said Lao Tze, the second saying sounds to me dangerous. To speak of 'loving all men' is a foolish exaggeration, and to make up one's mind to be impartial is in itself a kind of partiality. . . . You too shall learn to guide your steps by Inward Power, to follow the course that the Way of Nature sets; and soon you will reach a goal where you will no longer need to go round laboriously advertising goodness and duty, like the town-crier with his drum, seeking for news of a lost child. No Sir! What you are doing is to disjoint men's natures!" . . .
>
> "All this talk of goodness and duty, these perpetual pin-pricks, unnerve and irritate the hearer; nothing, indeed, could be more destructive of his inner tranquility. . . . The swan does not need a daily bath in order to remain white; the crow does not need a daily inking in order to remain black. . . . When the pool dries up, fish makes room for fish upon the dry land, they moisten one another with damp breath, spray one another with foam from their jaws. But how much better are they off when they can forget one another, in the freedom of river or lake!" [28]

Taoism's one piece of advice is that it has no advice to give. The French existentialist Gabriel Marcel observed that it is strangely impossible for a person to embark on a serious program of becoming a charming person. A person of great charm is precisely a relatively unselfconscious person, a matter which, as Marcel points out, accounts for the fact that small children are charming, or "natural." If one worked hard to become charming, the naturalness of the charm would turn itself into officious industry and reveal a self-conscious person working hard at playing the role of a natural, unselfconscious, charming person. It is impossible to make it a point to be charming. One simply is or is not.

Similarly, the serenity of those who enjoy mental

health can be ascribed to there being no need to take
extra thought about the healthy state of mind that they
thus enjoy "naturally." In fact, an over-self-consciousness
and overconcern with one's mental health (while
perhaps useful as a means of therapy) is, in fact, a sign of
its absence or incompleteness. In *Concluding Unscientific Postscript,* Kierkegaard has told the story of an
escapee from an insane asylum who in his desire to avoid
returning set himself the task of playing the role of a sane
man. Perhaps, he reasoned, he would appear sane if he
confined himself to statements he knew to be true, and
so he seized on the fact that the earth is round and
recited over and over as he walked, "Bang, the earth is
round." "Bang, the earth is round." Immediately as he
met his old friends, they and his physician could see that
he was still not cured of his insanity. But, added
Kierkegaard, in a fine distinction, "It is not to be thought
that the cure would consist in getting him to accept the
opinion that the earth is flat."[29] Taoism is not a matter of
deciding what one "ought" to do or what might be "true"
to think. The message of Taoism is that when one's
frame of mind is natural, that is, in accord with Tao, then
conscious, effortful decision is beside the point.

How can Taoism advise us to become natural when
natural is what we already are when we are not trying to
heed any advice? Ultimately, Taoism has no advice to
give and scorns intellectual and moral distinctions as
artificial: The Tao is, above all, natural. Busy advice on
how to attain Tao never suffices. "Be off with you! But
before you go I should like to remind you of what
happened to the child from Shouling that was sent to
Han-tan to learn the 'Han-tan Walk.' He failed to master
the steps, but spent so much time in trying to acquire
them that in the end he forgot how one usually walks,
and came home to Shou-ling crawling on all fours." The
Tao is attained by a natural effortlessness. Consider a
man relaxed by drunkenness who falls from a fast-driven
carriage. Why is he unharmed? "Neither death nor life,
astonishment nor fear can enter into his breast; therefore

when he bumps into things, he does not stiffen with
fright. If such integrity of the spirit can be got from wine,
how much greater must be the integrity that is got from
heaven?"[30]

When Mahayana Buddhism spread over the Eastern
world from India in the first few centuries of the
Christian Era, it arrived in China, through tradesmen
and Buddhist missionaries like Bodhidharma, and there
absorbed some of the Taoist elements of ancient Chinese
thought—paradox and quietism. That sect of Buddhism
called Zen hearkens back both to Mahayana Buddhism
and to Taoism. The word "Zen" derives from the Hindu
words for meditation, which are, in Sanskrit "Dhyana"
and in Pali "Jhana." In China these became "Ch'an" and
in Japan, "Zen." The founder of the Ch'an sect from
which Zen derives was Bodhidharma, an Indian monk
who traveled to China in the sixth century A.D. His
teaching bears some resemblance to Indian Vedantism
and is accordingly an extension of Mahayana rather than
Theravada Buddhism: The Buddha in every man's heart
is the sole reality. This Buddhahood can be realized only
by an intuition for which a preliminary discipline is a
help, but no use is found for books, images, or other
external aids. The point of our main interest in Zen is to
see how it addresses a problem that exists for mysticism
of all kinds, the problem that is stated with such charm
in Taoism: How does one teach someone what he needs
to know if both words (discursive knowing) and moral
injunctions are rejected?

In the Rinzai sect of Zen, the question of how to teach
in the absence of words with which to teach is answered
by its use of the *koan* as a kind of inducement to *satori*.
More than anyone else, D. T. Suzuki has attempted to
explain these two ideas to us Westerners, and what
follows is especially dependent on his examples. Satori,
he tells us, is an "intuitive looking into the nature of
things." Analogies to it are the sudden solution of a
mathematical problem, some new discovery that makes
one say "Eureka." It is, says Suzuki, like a mental

"revolution." It is "cataclysmic." Poetically expressed, it is like the "opening" of a flower or the "brightening up of the mind-works." "Satori" is not synonomous with the word "conversion," which has more of an emotional tone; Satori is simply "noetic." It is achieved not (according to Suzuki) by "quietism," that is, by simply sitting and sinking into torpidity. It is achieved when one arrives at "insight." Insight into what? Into "one's own Nature." And, it is clear, that one's own "Nature" is for Zen simply a different way of saying the "Nature" of Buddha.

> The Buddha is your own Mind, make no mistake to bow [to external objects]. "Buddha" is a Western word, and in this country [Japan] it means "enlightened nature"; and by "enlightened" is meant "spiritually enlightened." . . . This nature is the Mind, and the Mind is the Buddha, and the Buddha is the Way, and the Way is Zen. . . . Even if you are well learned in hundreds of the Sutras and Sastras, you still remain an ignoramus in Buddhism when you have not yet seen into your original Nature. Buddhism is not there [in mere learning]. The highest truth is unfathomably deep, is not the object of talk or discussion, and even the canonical texts have no way to bring it within reach.[31]

The koan, which is a mind-boggling puzzle, is the preferred method of the Rinzai sect for inducing insight, or satori. The apprentice in Zen is asked a question by his Zen master. The task of the apprentice is an odd one; it is to answer the question with a non sequitur, displaying logic in a broken state. In this way the young apprentice shows that the gate to his own nature swings open only when the intellect is checked. His "seeing into his own nature" (satori) comes not by means of intellect, not by any means at all; it comes *directly*. The master might ask, "Who is the Buddha?" to which the young man would reply, "Three *chin* of flax." "When not a thought is stirring in one's mind, is there any error here?" "As much as Mount Sumeru." A monk asked, "All things are said to be reducible to the One, but where is the One to be reduced?" The answer was, "When I was in the district of Ch'ing I had a robe made that weighed seven *chin*."[32] The irrationality of the koan stuns the mind's logical process so that it now "sees" things just as they are and not chopped up by logic. It is necessary, says Suzuki, to reach a psychological impasse in order to achieve satori. Here we could compare the role of existential anxiety and despair as a turning point in Christian conversion. One must drop into the abyss, hit bottom, before one knows who he is. Despair, for Kierkegaard and Tillich, is the "antechamber" of Christian faith or "the courage to be." It is like the condition of the "sick soul" described by William James. The soul that is brought to despair is also brought out of it. He is "twice-born."

Another method of instruction, *zazen*, or sitting meditation, is that preferred by the Soto Zen sect brought to Japan by Dogen (1200–1253). He established the headquarters and principle training center of Soto Zen in Eihei-ji located on a secluded mountainside on the Sea of Japan. It is still in use as a Zen monastery and is a place that attracts Japanese lay visitors who journey there on holiday pilgrimages. For the Soto sect, it is the sitting itself, rather than the koan, that is important. While Rinzai also, by our Western standards, puts a great deal of emphasis on sitting meditation, its main interest is the solution of the koan and the sudden awakening represented in satori. The Soto interpretation is that these intellectual puzzles are too active and purposive and that Buddhahood is achieved not so much in a sudden satori as by constant exercise without beginning and end.

Part of the exercises consists of sutra chanting, which is done in a monotonous rhythm and monotone to the percussive accompaniment of knockers, drums, and gongs. "Such music expresses a quite different religious intention from Christian religious music. It is meant to induce a state of trance-like meditation, absorbing the individual body and mind in an intense inward experience of religious truth from which awareness of everything external is excluded. It is not a hymn of praise, by which the creature lifts and offers himself to God."[33]

The experience of the Westerner who tries zazen is interestingly described by William Theodore De Bary in an account of his visit to Ehei-ji.

Since my hosts attached such supreme value to the sitting itself, a precise understanding of doctrinal issues was not prerequisite to getting on with the actual practice. They took me as I was, with no questions asked, and proceeded to instruct me in the techniques of zazen. Once one was poised, perfectly erect, on the cushion, the idea was to maintain the right balance of body and mind, at ease and yet not wholly relaxed; alert and on edge, yet not tense or tight. Proper control of breath was, of course, essential. As an exercise in this, I was told to inhale deeply, then incline slowly to one side (still straight instead of bending), and then, while exhaling gradually, return to center position. Next the same procedure on the other side; and so on, slowly back and forth, until one came to rest naturally and easily in an erect posture.

In such silence one realized how busy and noisy the mind is. But, having barely reached that realization, I suddenly became aware of a shadow moving across the wall as of someone approaching from behind. It was the Godo, the director of the monks' training. On his first such visit, he gave a good shove at the base of my spine to straighten me up; my posture left something to be desired. A while later he was back, and I felt a light tap on the shoulder, as of a rod being laid against it, followed by a sharp thwack with a real sting in it. . . .

When everyone had been knocked into line, there was stillness again. How long? It seemed an age, but I was no judge. My crossed legs ached and then grew numb. My dripping nose was an hourglass that never emptied, but with my finger tips in contact position on my lap, there was no way of fishing out a handkerchief. . . .

At the end I had to pry my frozen legs open with my hands and could barely rise to stand. To walk was out of the question. As the last man in, I was supposed to be the first man out, and the others in line behind me were waiting for me to move. Since no gesture of mine could induce them to precede me, I was finally forced to stumble through the door. Only after standing and jogging around a bit outside could I make my way unsteadily back to the hostel.[34]

Whatever the method, the goal of Hindu yoga and Buddhist meditation is enlightenment. Whatever the doctrine of man's nature and of reality, man's obligation is to know this real nature and how it relates to a reality partly hidden. No matter how theoretical, poetic, or technical the Indian religions become, their aim is to make effective a transformation of the self and the self's viewpoint. Whatever is taught, therefore, is taught with a practical end in view. But if enlightenment is the end, then surely there is presupposed a distinction between what is only apparently so and what is really so; and given that distinction, Indian religion becomes hospitable to mysticism. For Hinduism and Buddhism alike, man's situation is like that of Ramakrishna's little tiger who must learn who he is:

> The story is told of a tiger, great with young, who exhausted herself in search of food. Ravenously hungry, she sprang upon a herd of goats. In the violence of her leap, her birth pains began and, in giving birth, she died. The goats, who at first had scattered, now gathered around and took pity on the newborn tiger, whimpering at its mother's side. They adopted the cub and he grew up learning to bleat gently like a goat. Although his sharp teeth made it difficult, he learned to nibble the thin blades of grass like a goat. The vegetarian diet made him thin and meek. One night, when the young tiger had grown older, the herd was again attacked—this time by a fierce old male tiger. The goats scattered, but the little tiger-goat, devoid of fear, remained.
>
> Now, the male tiger, incensed at the little tiger's goatlike behavior, demanded: "What are you doing here among these goats? What are you doing chewing grass?" He seized the meek little tiger by the neck and forced him to look at his reflection in a pool of water. The fierce tiger carried him off to his den where he forced on him a piece of

bleeding, raw meat. The cub, though resistant, swallowed with a forced gulp. Then the little tiger began to feel at ease and gratified. A glowing strength went through his body. He smacked his lips and licked his jowls and yawned. Then, just as though he were waking from a sleep, from a night which had held him under a spell for years and years, he lashed his tail and let out a terrifying, triumphant roar. When the roar was finished, the old tiger said gruffly: "Now do you know what you really are?"[35]

One must learn to *see* the true nature of things, disguised though they are. Ultimately, the mystic's aim is *seeing*—a knowing which amounts to enlightenment. The mystic, however, must first *learn* to see; for in the beginning he cannot. He submits himself, therefore, to some preliminary discipline taught by his tradition. These are the techniques he must know "how" to do or know "about" as a prelude to his being able simply to "know" by direct enlightenment.

There are, then, in the mysticism of both East and West two modes of knowing. First, the mystic needs to know "about" the recommended techniques—the postures of meditation, the scripture and doctrine, the reasonings and the instructions. This is "know-how," or technical knowing; and in our next chapter, we shall adopt Plotinus' label for this way of knowing—*Epistēmē*. But there is an ultimate, nondiscursive, nontechnical way of knowing, which every mystic seeks by means of the particular discipline he practices. For its sake, he gladly throws away all techniques, no longer needing them. When one uses a brick to knock at a gate for entry (so a Zen Buddhist story goes), one can discard the brick when the gate is opened. The use of the brick (the koan) is technique, and one must have the "know-how" to use it. But this technical knowledge is not that which the mystic ultimately looks for. He looks rather for that which comes all at once when the gate swings open. Satori is the name which Zen Buddhism gives to this kind of knowing. In the next chapter, we shall find it called *Nous* by Plotinus. Differences of detail are important. *Nous* and *satori* are certainly not equivalent. Nevertheless, the mystics' enterprise is of one general pattern. The aim of mysticism is *ultimately* to know directly, and *preliminarily,* to do (or to know about) in order to know directly by *seeing.* Shortly we shall take a look at the pattern of mysticism as it is expressed by Christian mystics, especially Meister Eckhart and St. Teresa. Just now, we turn to see what forces give shape to the pattern of mysticism in its Christian form.

Chapter 3
Sources of Christian Mysticism

The apostle Paul's most notable failure as a preacher took place in Athens at the Areopagus, where, it is said in the book of Acts, men "spent their time in nothing except telling or hearing something new." Only two of his hearers "joined him and believed," but they are never mentioned again in the accounts of Paul's activities. The two were a woman named Damaris and a man called Dionysius the Areopagite. Nothing about them makes them important in themselves, but Dionysius the Areopagite, by an odd quirk of history, became the most important name in Western, medieval mysticism.

The story is this. A writer (whose true identity is unknown but who was probably a Syrian monk), in whom the ideas of Plotinus and Proclus as well as the mystery religions were influential, produced treatises on mystical theology in Greek, which in the ninth century A.D. were translated into Latin by John Scotus Erigena. These works were wrongly assumed to be the work of St. Paul's convert Dionysius the Areopagite and as a consequence were widely held to be authoritative among medieval theologians. "Dionysius" and Aristotle were chief authorities for St. Thomas Aquinas. The treatises, however, make use of Neoplatonist thought forms that would represent an anachronism for a Pauline convert, so that in discussions of mysticism today, it is customary to refer to the writer, by one of the most unwieldy names in theology: he is called "Pseudo-Dionysius, the Areopagite." (We might enter the cautionary word that Pseudo-Dionysius is not to be confused with the Greek god Dionysus, or Zagreus. The adjective, Dionysian, is sometimes confusingly used of both.)

Pseudo-Dionysius is in fact responsible for the word "mysticism" as a name for what was called "contemplation" prior to his influence. The treatises of Pseudo-Dionysius represent a strongly speculative type of mysticism, of which we shall say more shortly. The story of his name illustrates the fact that Western mysticism is a complex of several components that do not harmonize easily. These components are (a) biblical literature, (b) mystery religions, and (c) Greek philosophy, especially Neoplatonism.

Mysticism and Biblical Literature

In assaying biblical literature for traces of the mystical element, the results are ambiguous. Part of the ambiguity lies in the word "mystical" itself, and part lies in the complexity of the Bible and its interpretation.

The word "mystical" can be simply another name for "religious" or "religiously responsive." While this is a legitimate use of the word, it is the least helpful way to speak about mysticism because it does not serve to distinguish it from religion itself. Often the idea of immediacy is stressed in this conception of the mystical, so that one who sees a vision of God or "hears" God is said to be "mystical." In this broadest sense, the Bible is throughout mystical. Moses, the prophets, Jesus, and Paul—all would be "mystics."

If, however, we take our clue about what is mystical from the medieval speculative mystics, then mysticism is a way of thought, a world view of a certain pattern largely dependent on Neoplatonist sources. What will we look for if we seek mysticism in this sense? We should look for reality as an undifferentiated Unity, ultimately inde-

scribable in words, and we should look for kinship
between man and God described in metaphors that tend
to obscure the distinction: Man is like a drop of water;
God like the ocean. Ultimately, man's soul and God
commingle and become identical. What of man's religious obligation? It is to turn from the world and be
reunited with God, the One. His ethical task? Ultimately,
he does not have one. As a preliminary, there are things
man ought to do, but from the standpoint of the
undifferentiated Unity, deeds and decisions are not
ultimately significant. Whatever is mystical in this sense
tends to do away with particulars in the interest of a
broader, more universal, ultimately undifferentiated
Unity. The concrete, the historical, the factual, and the
ethical are particulars that get left behind. It is this
universalizing feature of mysticism that we need to focus
on in assessing the Bible for a mystical element.

A part of the difficulty of arriving at a clear result,
however, comes from the Bible itself. Does the Bible have
in it this universalizing feature of mysticism? An earlier
phase of interpretation wished to say that it had and also
to emphasize it. That was the phase of liberal theology
associated with Albert Schweitzer's Christ mysticism
and with Harnack's *Essence of Christianity*. It looked to
the essence of Christianity as a religion that underlay the
historical particulars. Later interpreters repudiated this
enterprise and found that the essence of "biblical" faith
lay in its concreteness rather than its universality. This
was the program of neo-orthodoxy. Its interest in the
"uniqueness" and particularity of the Christian revelation led it to minimize any universalizing features in the
biblical literature. Neither the liberals nor the neo-
orthodox had mysticism as a major preoccupation, but
the fact that neo-orthodoxy renounced the earlier
interest in the universalizing features of the Bible meant
that it also strongly renounced mysticism. Typically, it
drew the sharpest contrast between that which is Greek
and universalizing and that which is biblical and

concrete. Sam Keen in *Apology for Wonder* gives a handy standard schema showing the contrast as maximal. The following is an abbreviation of that schema.[1]

Greek Thought	*Hebrew-Christian Thought*
Centered in experience of nature—philosophical.	Centered in the experience of history—theological.
Anthropocentric or cosmocentric—reason is the essence of man.	Theocentric—being addressed by God and responding in faith is the essence of man.
Abstract, universal, conceptual patterns of thought are dominant. Thought aims at attaining static, nonhistorical, metaphysical truths.	Concrete, particular, dramatic patterns of thought are dominant. Thought aims at grasping dynamic historical realities.
The highest form of love is *eros,* which is love recognizing value in its object.	*Agape* is the highest form of love, a self-giving form of love.
Rooted in attitudes of ontological, theoretical, and cosmological wonder.	Rooted in historical wonders.

When the contrast is made absolute between Greek ways of thought and Hebrew-Christian ways of thought, the contrast between what is biblical and what is mystical is also overdrawn, so that what is mystical is depicted as an essentially Greek orientation involving a spiritual quest initiated by man, and what is biblical, as entirely God's initiative on behalf of man. The Bible is interpreted as a "recital" of the mighty acts of God in history.

It is far too simple to say, however, what in the aftermath of neo-orthodoxy has often been said, that whatever is biblical is not mystical. For one thing, there simply is a universalizing strand in the Bible, so that while the Bible may not be mystical, it does contain one element of the mystical. For another, the writings of

Western mystics were thoroughly saturated with biblical texts, so that by intention, at least, the mystics do not mean to say anything that runs counter to what is biblical. To be sure, they often simply "used" biblical texts to illustrate ideas drawn from Neoplatonist sources, and they do not hesitate to give themselves amazingly wide latitude in interpreting the texts. Thus Eckhart:

> Dionysius says: "God has no idea of himself and no likeness, for he is intrinsic good, truth, and being." God does all that he does within himself and of himself in an instant. Do not imagine that when God made heaven and earth and all the creatures, that he made one today and another tomorrow. To be sure, Moses describes it thus, but he knew much better! He put it this way on account of the people who could neither understand nor conceive it otherwise.[2]

Obviously Eckhart has allowed his Neoplatonist ontology to overtake Moses.

The Two Strands. The question of what is mystical and what is nonmystical in the biblical tradition cannot be answered with finality because to do so is to ask that two strands that lie essentially joined in the biblical tradition be loosened one from another, when the loosening would be destructive of the biblical tradition itself—a separation of the wheat and the tares. One of the biblical strands is a strong *ethical* interest that exists in the New Testament as well as in the Old, and which makes every decision urgent, a matter of being for or against. With the ethical content, man is placed in the position of *decision.* He is faced with an either-or disjunction. If he decides for this, he decides against that. This radical ethical disjunction is incompatible with the ultimate vision of mysticism, which goes beyond moral distinctions and assumes that what the world calls goodness is too small a category for that which cannot be categorized at all—the One. Alongside this ethical decisiveness in the Bible there is a *universalizing* strand, a vision and indeed a bestowing of accepting love that is so all-encompassing that nothing, and especially not a wrong ethical decision, can tip the scales, finally, against it. It is certainly the universalizing rather than ethical strand that is most congenial to the ultimate vision of mysticism.

Biblical religion is not ethical in the sense of being preoccupied with the inherent "goodness" residing within man. It is "ethical" in the crucial importance it gives to what men *do* as they relate themselves to a God who takes an active role in their lives. The Bible depicts man in the Garden of Eden in terms of the overwhelming importance it attaches to what he *does* there. He is given sanctions and prohibitions. He is tempted, by virtue of the ethical freedom he experiences. He decides to override the prohibition, and he loses his primitive innocence. His depravity occasions the wrath of God and the Flood. Eventually, as a benefaction to man, a covenant is made between man and God. Now man knows where he stands and what he *ought* to do. There is a new moral orderliness in the world, and man is assured that his relationship with God is trustworthy and not haphazard. God will keep his side of the bargain if man will keep his—and men were not so sure God trustworthy in this way before the covenant. Yet even this Mosaic covenant is twisted by the stiff-necked disobedience and self-serving cunning of men, and as a result, the fury of God is unleashed against them for allowing the covenant to become narrow and formalistic, subject to casuistry and self-serving ends.

> I hate, I despise your feasts,
>   and I take no delight in your solemn
>   assemblies.
> Even though you offer me your burnt
>   offerings and cereal offerings,
>   I will not accept them. . . .
> Take away from me the noise of your songs; . . .
>   I will not listen.
> But let justice roll down like waters,
>   and righteousness like an everflowing stream.
>   (Amos 5:21-24)

In voices of moral outrage, the prophets called for a radical change. The false prophets and the priests had dealt falsely with the Old Covenant: "The false pen of the scribes has made it into a lie" (Jer. 8:8). "They have healed the wound of my people lightly" (Jer. 8:11). The radical reform demanded a "new covenant," not like the old—subject to scribal casuistry—but one written "upon their hearts" (Jer. 31:31-33).

Now there must be a *universalizing* of man's relationship to God. All men, since they have hearts and stand in need of forgiveness, can "know" God as the bestower of forgiveness without having the relationship bestowed by the expert: "And no longer shall each man teach his neighbor and each his brother, saying, 'Know the Lord,' for they shall all know me, from the least of them to the greatest, says the Lord; for I will forgive their iniquity, and I will remember their sin no more" (Jer. 31:34).

Jesus, historically considered, stands in the line of the prophets. He scorned empty ceremony and expressed the prophets' concern for the poor and outcast; he had the prophetic insistence on the interiority of obedience and the same conviction of universality of mankind under the fatherhood of God. "The sabbath was made for man, not man for the sabbath" (Mark 2:27).

Is prophetic religion a mystical type of religion or not? This question is not easy to answer for the reason that the prophets, above all, are imbued with a nonmystical, moral decisiveness; yet their relationship with God is surely a *direct* one and not mediated to them by means of the priestly institutional conduits, which are frequently the object of their criticisms. Their authority for speaking in the name of Yahweh derives from a more direct source than the priestly hierarchy. In a sense, it is possible to say that there is a mystical element in prophetic religion if by that we mean that the man-God relationship is immediate, unchanneled through "established" institutions like the priestly offices, and that it can embrace all men universally. Yet this simple immediacy is not mysticism in the same sense as the later Neoplatonist mysticism.

For Moses and the prophets, immediate access to God meant that they were conversant with him. They "heard" and proclaimed his "word." The Neoplatonist mystics understood the immediacy of the relationship in analogies drawn from nature that made the soul and God identical. The prophet senses an overwhelming moral obligation to be obedient to his commission. There is something that he as a personality must *do,* and typically he is discomforted by the obligation and initially resistant to it. The mystic, on the other hand, does not see his relationship with God ultimately in moral terms at all. Initially, he sees it in terms of kinship, ultimately in terms of identity. The mystic may, and often does, *do* things and change things for the better, but his moral and reforming efforts are a by-product of his ultimate aim, "union" with God. The most that can be said is that prophetism has some mystical elements—immediacy, interiority, and universalizing love—but because of its ethical decisiveness, it cannot be of one piece with later medieval mysticism.

The situation is also complex in the case of the apostle Paul, in whom the ethical and the universal are also found woven together. Even Paul's Epistles contain many injunctions to do the "right" things, to do what one "ought" despite his general view that the law is the yoke of slavery while the gospel is liberating. Those led by the Spirit, he says, must strenuously avoid the "works of the flesh," and Paul gives a morally bracing list: "Immorality, impurity, licentiousness, idolatry, sorcery, enmity, strife, jealousy, anger, selfishness, dissension, party spirit, envy, drunkenness, carousing, and the like. . . . Those who do such things shall not inherit the kingdom of God" (Gal. 5:19-21). But the distinction Paul seems to make is in the *motive* one has for eschewing the works of the flesh. Obedience flows from faith; faith is not a moral virtue achieved at the successful outcome of a kind of moral contest within one's soul.

Alongside the biblical ethical interest, there is a universalizing strand, a vision of accepting love that is so encompassing that nothing is rejected by it, and this is a theme of the Old Testament as well as the New; for it has been a profound disservice to Judaism that Christians have been content to think of the giving of the Torah as a burden rather than a gift of love. But certainly the theme of universal love is concentrated in the New Testament especially in the Pauline Epistles. For when Paul asks what might separate man from the love of God, the message of assurance is overwhelmingly persuasive for him: "For I am sure that neither death, nor life, nor angels, nor principalities, nor things present, nor things to come, nor powers, nor height, nor depth, nor anything else in all creation, will be able to separate us from the love of God in Christ Jesus our Lord" (Rom. 8:38-9).[3]

Similar is the comforting, all-embracing love announced by Jesus in Matthew: "Come to me, all who labor and are heavy laden, and I will give you rest. Take my yoke upon you, and learn from me; for I am gentle and lowly in heart, and you will find rest for your souls. For my yoke is easy, and my burden is light" (Matt. 11:28-30).

Another and perhaps the most important example of the universalizing strand in the Bible is illustrated in the development in the interpretation of the role of Jesus that is evident in the New Testament. The transition may be summarized, rather glibly, as a drift from an historical "Jesus movement" to a Christ mysticism.

Jesus is presented in the Gospels in part as a teacher, as one called Rabbi. He is one who has a "new teaching" (Mark 1:27), one followed by people who crowd around wherever he speaks. His teaching is the imminent coming of a new relationship between God and man, one that has indeed begun to exist already. The relationship is understood in the analogy of *Kingdom,* a term that had political overtones for many of Jesus' followers. He himself may have meant to convey the more general notion of rule or dominion. His descriptions of what this kingdom is like have to do with the family in which trust, love and forgiveness prevail—the parable of the prodigal son is the noteworthy example.

The shock of Jesus' death gave impetus to a new interpretation of his role. Now Jesus' mission is reinterpreted in a way that does not confine his influence to the historical period in which he lived and taught but universalizes his influence and transcends *all* times and *all* places. This new conception is summarized in the "resurrection faith" expressed, for example, by the early preaching of Peter recorded in Acts: "God has made him both Lord and Christ, this Jesus whom you crucified" (Acts 2:36). Now Jesus becomes, not merely a "founder" of a band of followers, but "Christ," the transcendent focus of faith for all times and places.

This change removes the embarrassment for Christians who happen to live at the wrong time and in the wrong place—Paul especially, who as one born "out of time" could nevertheless claim authority to preach the gospel of Christ because his authority flowed not from men but from "revelation of Jesus Christ" (Gal. 1:12). In other words, his authority was direct and did not depend on institutional channels. Now man's redemption is viewed in the analogy of *dying* to sin and *rising again* to a new life in the spirit (I Cor. 15:12). This capacity to die to sin and to the old and to live again to the new life is either conferred by Christ's own resurrection or is perhaps another way of thinking of Christ's resurrection itself (I Cor. 15:16). Man's ethical life is now reinterpreted as a relationship to Christ seen as a Cosmic Principle—a Gospel addressed to all men and therefore of universal applicability to the human condition. Needless to say St. Paul's missionary activity throughout the Mediterranean world made this universalism a practical and concrete experience.

Of all the biblical books, John's Gospel is, in its universalizing tendency, in its shift of gaze from the historical Jesus and his followers to a cosmic Christ, the most mystical. That is not to say, however, that the strictly ethical interest is lacking; the command to love one another is especially the emphasis of this Gospel. Jesus is now understood as the *Logos,* as an eternal principle, the "Word" through which everything was created. For some early readers of the Fourth Gospel, Logos would summon associations connected with its use first by Heraclitus and then (in the form *Nous*) by Plato and Aristotle. The Stoics referred to Logos and made it the rational and, in fact, the material principle of the cosmos.

> In the beginning was the Word, and the Word was with God, and the Word was God. He was in the beginning with God; all things were made through him, and without him was not anything made that was made. In him was life, and the life was the light of men. The light shines in the darkness, and the darkness has not overcome it.
>
> (John 1:1-9)

The language is strange. Whatever the Evangelist intended by it, its import for mysticism is the use of an abstract and universal principle, Logos, to understand "who Jesus was." It is not said that Jesus was a carpenter of Nazareth. It is said that Jesus, the Christ, is the rational principle that thinkers like Plato, Aristotle, and the Stoics had always held had bound all things together. This emphasis in John's Gospel means that we are to look for continuity between nature (creation) and Spirit. Revelation is, in one sense, a manifestation of what had been present all along. The meaning of Christ interpreted as Logos is that everything, in being what it is, is symbolic of something "more," and that Christ is discerned, not only by looking to the Galilean ministry, but by seeking the "true" nature of all things and men everywhere.[4]

The Mystics' Use of the Bible. The mystics themselves had favorite biblical allusions that seemed to illustrate their own contemplative disposition and life. In the Old Testament, they often cited the ascent of Moses to Mt. Sinai and the direct accessibility of God to him there. It was not Moses' acquisition of the law that interested

them, but the ascent (which they treated as analogous to
the *via purgativa*) and its culmination in an immediate
experience of God. The Song of Songs contributed the
vocabulary of romantic love to the mystics' personal
religious devotions. In the light of post-Freudian
psychology, it is apparent that the language of love
became tinged with sexuality—one need only consider
such expressions as the "bride of Christ," "spiritual
marriage," rapture, et cetera. Protestantism has been
especially uncomfortable with such language,
"warmed," as Nietzsche observed, by celibacy. Indeed,
St. Bernard of Clairvaux, who is most famous for his
treatise on the Song of Songs and for the mystical
development of the idea of love, had to enjoin his monks
to listen to his instruction with "chaste" ears. While this
vocabulary makes the mystics a happy hunting ground
for psychological investigation, it did succeed in expressing the human and personal relationship between God
and man that the mystics seemed to experience. It
opened the way to a personal and practical mysticism,
lyrical in nature, with beautiful literary and devotional
possibilities. It placed the mystics' spirit at the farthest
remove from Neoplatonist speculation and made it
personal and warm.

In the New Testament two incidents especially
interested the mystics. The conversion experience of
Paul on the road to Damascus seemed to them analogous
to the soul's absorption in God, "caught up to the third
heaven—whether in the body or out of the body I do not
know" (II Cor. 12:3). The other New Testament incident
popular with the mystics as an illustration was the story
of Mary and Martha (Luke 10:38-42). Of the two sisters,
Mary, the "contemplative," had, said Jesus, "chosen the
good portion," the more permanent, enduring value,
which could not "be taken away from her." Martha, the
practical housekeeper, represented the *distractions* of
the active (as opposed to the contemplative) values. A
famous extended homily (and tribute to Mary) appears in
the fourteenth-century English devotional classic *The*

Cloud of Unknowing.[5] St. Teresa and St. Bernard of Clairvaux, on the other hand, wish to give realism its due; they grant an important place to the active, practical life. The story of Mary and Martha provided the mystics with an analogue for the tension between the active and contemplative claims upon their lives.

We conclude that it is quite wrong to use *biblical* and *mystical* as if they were antithetical terms. To do so is to overlook the complex nature of mysticism and of the Bible itself. There are elements in the Bible that are incompatible with mysticism, and these are largely the components of its strong ethical emphasis. The righteous indignation of prophetism is entirely too decisive for the mystics, who, in the interests of an ultimate unity, are diffident about making any distinctions, even moral ones. Yet the words of forgiveness, recovery, and return in the Bible itself point to a relationship of love between man and God in which the distinction of good and evil does not have the final say. As Paul put it in Romans 5:7-8: "Why, one will hardly die for a righteous man—though perhaps for a good man one will dare even to die. But God shows his love for us in that while we were yet sinners Christ died for us." To be sure, in the Bible, reconciliation is a familial one, like that which occurs in the story of the prodigal son, and it is never expressed metaphysically as "absorption." Nevertheless, the word of forgiveness and reconciliation makes impermanent the distinction between good deeds and bad deeds and transmutes a narrow, moralistic outlook into a universal gesture of welcoming love that embraces men in all times and in all places.

The Mystery Religions

When one says "mystery religions," one refers to a cluster of cults which became popular in the Mediterranean world around the second century B.C. Their origin is apparently impossible to trace, since similar myths existed from ancient times in Sumer, Egypt, Syria, Greece, and elsewhere. The first Christian missions were undertaken in an environment in which these mystery cults were highly influential, and it was natural for Paul and the early church fathers to express themselves in symbols that formed a part of the experience of their hearers. The mystery religions thus provided a matrix of communication, even though both Paul (in his correspondence with Corinth) and the fathers had to show wherein Christianity was different from the antinomianism of the cults.

Generally, these cults—as they were practiced in Hellenistic times—represented a shift from religion as a civic duty to religion as an intimate act of personal devotion. They were, in contrast to the old Roman civic religions, "less mindful of economic utility" and more directed toward an "inner spirit." They could cause "emotions, stronger than any rational faculty, to gush forth from the depths of the soul."[6] The aim of these mysteries, achievement of an identity of the self with the divine, is expressed in the myths and cultic practices surrounding various dying and reviving gods: Osiris in Egypt; Adonis in Syria; Demeter, Dionysus, Orpheus in Greece; Mithra in Persia and the Roman world. They flourished in the Mediterranean world in the Hellenistic age inaugurated by the conquests of Alexander the Great (ca. 323 B.C.). They presented the opportunity for the initiate to see divine possibilities in himself that could be set free simply by means of his identification with the god.

Although the names of the gods and the ritual details differed, all these cults had certain features in common.[7] These were: (1) the sharing of a secret rite by which members were initiated into a community and through which sharing the sense of community was enhanced; (2) rites of purification—fasting or baptism, for example—that preceded initiation; (3) disclosure of the secret formula; (4) vision of the deity by the initiate; and (5) union with the deity. The initiate might also be vested with the robe of the god, that is, "put on" the deity and eat a sacred meal that effects communion with him.

The aim of the mysteries was thus to express in cultic practice the affinity between the individual soul and the divine spirit—a function called *deification* and certainly a major theme for Christian mystics. Whether or not Christian mystics assumed the outright identity of God and soul is debatable and has been a special bone of contention between mystics and those in charge of doctrinal purity. But mystics like St. Teresa and Meister Eckhart were fond of quoting Paul's speech in Galatians 2:20: "I have been crucified with Christ; it is no longer I who live, but Christ who lives in me"; and more often than not, they interpreted the words in a way (which modern commentators disavow) to mean that the *I* is totally displaced by Christ. In fact, one of the aberrant characteristics of the mystics' view of the man-God relationship was the acceptance of a simple deification process by which the self must be supplanted altogether by a higher spirit. This belief sometimes resulted in ruthless suppression of all self-interest and fanatical asceticism.

In any event, several ideas flow into Christian mysticism from the mystery cults:[8] First of all, Christian mysticism—especially in its nonspeculative, lyrical, and devotional form—has an intensity of fervor and personalness that locates it, with the mysteries, light years beyond a perfunctory state religion. Second, there is in the mysteries, as well as in Christian mysticism, the sense of the unspeakableness and secrecy of the religious "knowledge" that is disclosed. The word "mysticism," in fact, derives from the Greek *muein,* "to keep mum," used in connection with the mysteries. Third, there is the assumption common to the mysteries and Christian mysticism that the spiritual pilgrimage involves three stages—a stage of ascetic purification as a preparation, a stage of illumination, and a final stage of union. Fourth, the idea of deification was certainly a part of the mysteries and was one of the ways in which the Christian mystics thought about the man-God relation: the soul, in its spiritual journey, was assumed to become more and more Godlike. The question for Christian piety, however, was how to attribute divinity to the soul of man without overstepping the bounds of humility. The extravagances of Eckhart, in this regard, set the scene for the condemnation of his teaching by the institutional church.

Dean Inge has suggested two ways of thinking of the idea of deification.[9] One way, which he calls "substitution," stresses man's present alienation and his need for redemption. Man on his own is in a bad way. He cannot save himself; his salvation must come from a source *oustide* himself. This is a less philosophical, a more practical and soteriological view. This, according to Inge, is the view implied in the activity of the mystery cults, which were intended to impart salvation to man in need of it. Here, man *acquires* divine attributes from a deity who *bestows* them. In the second way, which Inge calls "essentialism," man is assumed to have divine attributes already hidden within himself from the beginning. These need only be brought to the surface.

Of these two ways, speculative mysticism, as it was expressed philosophically in Neoplatonism seems more allied with the second, essentialist way of seeing deification of human nature. Let us briefly consider the influence of this school.

Greek Philosophy

When the mystics explained themselves in theoretical language, they drew almost entirely upon the Neoplatonist tradition in philosophy, the sources of which are found in Plato himself, in Aristotle's *Metaphysics,* in Plotinus and Pseudo-Dionysius.[10] This tradition, as the mystics put it to use, provided a set of common assumptions about human nature and its destiny. Man belongs to two worlds. He is an earthly being and as such has something to overcome; a part of his nature is resistant to good, an obstacle to his loftier aspirations. Yet a higher, originally divine part of his nature is akin to that which is highest in the world—the sphere of ideas, of thought, of God. What man must do is liberate this better part of himself from its entanglement with the worse part. The mystery cults provided a liturgical means for the liberation; philosophy provided the avenue of thought, of intellectual love, and of lofty idealism. The philosopher, above all, is one who can discern the misjudgments of the world and correct its course. The common assumptions in what we can broadly term Platonism were a dualistic view of the world and of human nature, unchangeableness as the standard of reality, and a program of ascetic and intellectual self-fulfillment.

The Orphic Myth of Zagreus (Dionysus). At the base of the Platonist tradition was an ancient Orphic myth influential in Plato himself. The myth tells us of Zagreus (Dionysus), who was the son of Zeus and Persephone. Zeus had decided to give the world to Zagreus as his kingdom, but when Zagreus was still a child, he was kidnapped by the Titans, who enticed him with toys. They tore him to pieces and devoured him. With his famous thunderbolt, Zeus then destroyed the Titans, burning them to ashes. Zeus used these same ashes as his material to create man. The raw material of man's nature is thus a mixture of good and evil. Since the ashes were of the Titans, man is made from rebellious, wicked stuff; but since the Titans had consumed something divine, Zagreus, their ashes were also in part divine. Man, then, is a mixture of good and evil. There is a divinity in all men that is entrapped but not destroyed by the evil outer wrapping. Men are condemned by their impurity to a cycle of births and deaths—a transmigration of souls or reincarnation—the same idea that exists in Hinduism. They can escape this fate by the purification rites of the mysteries.

Plato. The Zagreus myth is a poetic, mythic way of characterizing the nature of man. Plato's philosophy does not differ essentially from the Zagreus myth in its diagnosis of man's condition. What Plato adds is a new remedy. *Knowledge,* not liturgical purification, delivers

man's soul from the prison house of the body and
restores man to his divine origin. It is man's ignorance of
his origin that keeps him in thrall. But, having deep
inside him the inherent divine spark and memory of his
previous existence, man also has inside him the
motivating power (*Eros*) to regain his home and to
perceive his true identity. Knowledge of the truth is,
therefore, a recollection (*anamnesis*), and teaching is,
therefore, a matter of reminding one of what he knows
already but has, for the time, forgotten. It is preeminently
the role of the philosopher to teach by reminding men of
that better, truer world that their present existence
makes them forget.

In the allegory of the cave in Plato's *Republic,* man's
situation of ignorance is compared to the condition of
men fastened in an underground cave. Facing one wall,
they are chained at their necks and legs in such a way
that they cannot turn their heads to see one another or
anything else directly. What they do see are shadows of
vessels and various things that are carried before the
light of a fire and thus shown in outline on their wall.
The things themselves they have never seen. Now if they
are released and gain direct sight of the objects, they will
misinterpret them. They will wrongly assume that this
new world they see for the first time is less real than the
shadowy objects they were used to. The philosopher is
one who has gotten rid of such chains and climbed out of
the dark cave into the light of day. He knows that the
true reality is found in this upper world and that the
sense world is related to this upper, real world as shadow
is to the real object. But to know this man must undergo
a painful conversion. Relinquishing old habits of thought
is as painful as turning around is painful to prisoners
whose muscles have stiffened. If they undergo the
discipline, what they leave behind is the transitory, the
fleeting and the illusory; what they gain is the eternal
and the real.

"This world" is shadowy but "that world" is real and
divine. Fortunately, according to Plato, even after the

soul fell into its body "like an oyster in his shell" (*Phaedrus* 250), it retains a memory of "that world" and feels an attraction to it which it cannot fully understand. In Plato's *Phaedrus,* we learn that some souls have better memories than others. These are the wiser and more noble souls. The "wings" of their souls are strong, and they make their way upward and homeward with less difficulty. But every soul can improve its memory of its origin by perceiving beauty and awakening to Absolute Beauty. In the *Symposium,* we are told that a spiritual form of love, Eros, is man's motivating power to strive for purer and purer forms until he reaches Absolute Beauty. In both dialogues, man's task is described as an *ascent*—the Platonist symbol so frequently used by the mystics.

Aristotle and the Changelessness of God. As Plato described it, man's motivating power in his lofty aspiration is Eros, the impulse to acquire that higher thing which is lacking. We need to notice that having love (Eros) implies that there is some unmet need, some lack on the part of man. Eros is like a pulley drawn between a need and its fulfillment. In the *Symposium,* this tension in Eros is depicted mythically by making Eros the son of Penia (poverty) and Poros (plenty).

This presence of need or lack in Eros greatly influences the way one thinks of God or the gods when one adopts the Platonist world view. Since God cannot be supposed to lack anything, he cannot be supposed to love either. There is nothing toward which God needs to move, nothing he needs to possess that he does not already have, nothing he needs to become that he is not already. There is no unrealized potential in God (Aristotle *Metaphysics* XII, 1072b5). He is, as the scholastics expressed it, pure actuality—*actus purus* and *a se,* or self-sufficient. Eros love is not an emotional feeling but a movement toward self-fulfillment. God, who is already perfectly fulfilled, cannot, therefore, love. Such is the outcome when one applies Book XII of Aristotle's *Metaphysics* to Christian conceptions of God. God must take no notice of anything not of God. He must think only of that which is worthy of his thought, and that is thought itself. Here we have come the greatest distance from biblical conceptions of God. The necessary changelessness and aseity of God was an enormously influential idea among the speculative Christian mystics, and it made it ultimately impossible for those like Eckhart to reconcile their thoughts of God with the Bible.

Another similar difficulty in Christianizing Aristotle's *Metaphysics* was that man is thrown largely on his own resources and inherent capacity. No divine assistance is forthcoming for him. With Aristotle (and with Plato) no conception of grace could work itself in. Aristotle held that all individual things, with the exception of God of course, have a natural development toward an end (*telos*). An acorn becomes an oak tree; a child becomes a man; copper becomes a bowl. Every individual thing in the world has an end. God, as the Unmoved Mover of all these processes, moves them—not directly as an efficient cause—but only as a final cause or end. God moves the world, not by his own initiative, but by being "loved" by the world itself (*Metaphysics* XII, 1072b). Man's task is to become *really* what he is only *implicitly*. He is inspired by a vision of his true end but his resources lie wholly in himself—in his intellectual aspiration and his moral courage.

Neoplatonism: The Philosophy of Plotinus and His School. The Christian mystics who drew on both biblical and Platonist sources, needed somehow to reconcile the living God of the Bible with the self-contained God of Aristotle. The reconciliation, never complete, was in some ways aided by the visual imagery by which Plotinus depicted the relationship between Divine Spirit and the world. Plato had especially emphasized ascent—the flight of the soul to the highest reality. The initiative took place with man. The special feature that Plotinus added was an outflow (emanation) from the divine source toward man and the world. Plotinus thus allowed for some receptivity on the part of man. The idea of

Christian grace could now find a niche in Platonism. To be sure, in following Plotinus, the mystic interpretation of grace was sometimes too naturalistic and deterministic.

Plotinus has us visualize a spiritual source of energy, value, and being which he simply calls the One. We can think of this divine influence by picturing a central source of light like the sun emitting rays with lessening intensity until the outer edges fade to dimness and then to darkness. Or perhaps we can envision a perpetually bubbling spring emitting concentric ripples until stillness prevails at the outermost ring of water. Man, the world, and everything in it is to be understood in terms of its relative distance from this original, wholly spiritual source called the One. Plotinus named the several gradations of intensity *hypostases* of being. And the Christian mystics derived their hierarchical view of the world from Plotinus' levels of being.

Closest to the One and most divine of the hypostases is *Nous* (Spirit or Intelligence), signifying nondiscursive reason or pure contemplation. Next is Soul *(Psyche)*, which is the animating principle of the whole universe as well as of man individually. "As the rays of the sun light up and gild a dark cloud, so the soul by entering the body of the universe gives it life and immortality and awakens it from inertia. . . . The presence of the soul gives the universe its value while before it was no more than an inert corpse" *(Ennead* V, 1).[11] Soul, as with Plato, has a nostalgic instinct to return to its origin, but it also has something of its original light to shine upon lower forms. Body, or Nature *(Physis)*, is the stuff which Soul animates and invests with value. And, at the lowest rung, is Matter, which is unilluminated by the One and is therefore without being or value—a nothing.

Although it is impossible to picture Plotinus' world view without thinking of motion and cause and effect, Plotinus was as strict as Aristotle in insisting that this divine influence is brought to bear without any activity on the part of the divine source itself and without its diminishing itself. Do not, he said, think of it literally as a process in time, for "we are treating of eternal things" and speaking metaphorically. The One influences the world without undergoing any change itself, just "as the brilliant light which surrounds and emanates perpetually from the sun does not affect its self-same and unchanging existence" *(Ennead* V, 1).[12]

Needless to say Plotinus (and the Christian mystics when they followed him) found ordinary language greatly strained by such a vision. Little can be said to describe the One except to say that it is the perfect source—eternally perfect and eternally productive *(Ennead* V, 1).[13] If much else is said, if it is defined, then the One becomes a one among other members of a class of things instead of the originating source of everything that takes precedence over all. The One cannot be spoken of or even known in the same way that derived, ordinary things are known. "When we wish to speak with precision," Plotinus said, "we should not say that the One is this or that. We must, as we 'revolve' around it, try to express what we feel in regard to it. We must do this in the light of the experiences we undergo when at times we approach the One and then again withdraw from it as a result of the difficulties involved" *(Ennead* VI, 9).[14]

Reason in Plotinus and Pseudo-Dionysius. The strain that occurs in language does not signal for Plotinus the collapse of rationality. Rather, it signals a shift to a higher form of reason. Just as there are levels of being, there are levels of reason. There is *reason* and there is *reasoning*. The highest reason, Nous, is nondiscursive. It is a vision of that which is single, the One. The lower forms, *dianoia* and *epistēmē* (dialectic and science), are a discursive *reasoning* directed toward the multiplicity of things.

Distinguishing reason in its discursive form as reasoning and thus isolating it from its nondiscursive, intuitive form is unnatural to the modern mind, which tends to limit being "reasonable" to a technical operation of problem-solving, that is determining the factors and

priorities and "sorting out" possible solutions. Reasoning
in this sense is precisely sorting, which is to say, seeing
the proper order in a multiplicity of things. The modern
mind more often than not labels any intuitive grasp of a
thing "irrational" because by and large it limits the word
"reason" to the proper application of some technique—in
the manner of engineering, for example. But engineering is a modern example of discursive reason in its
technological application. Plotinus's view of it was a
sorting out of *ideas* rather than operations—the *dialectic*
for which Socrates was so famous. Even as Plotinus
describes dialectic, however, it is still a sorting out of a
multiplicity of things, and as such it falls short of a vision
of pure unity itself.

> It is an art of reasoning which makes us capable to say
> about each thing what it is, in what it differs from other
> things, in what it resembles them, what its context is and
> proper function in this context, and whether existence
> belongs to it. It enables us to say into how many kinds
> Being falls and to distinguish Being from that which is not
> Being.[15]

It is not to be assumed that Plotinus denigrated this
discursive use of reason. He regarded it, in fact, as the
highest form of philosophy; but since it deals with a
multiplicity, it simply must "stop" or "pause," as he says,
when it arrives at unity and finds it needs to contemplate
it. "For how can we represent as different from us that
which did not seem, while we were contemplating it,
other than ourselves but in perfect at-oneness with us"
(*Ennead* VI, 9)?[16] And he adds, interestingly, that this
difficulty of language, no doubt, is the explanation
behind the secrecy of the mystery rites. Since that which
is divine is inexpressible, the initiate is forbidden to talk
of it to anyone who has not experienced it.

The graduated, hierarchical schema in Plotinus was a
way of doing justice to transcendence without altogether
removing Divinity from man's access and knowledge.

Pseudo-Dionysius pushes the One (God) beyond man's rational reach altogether.

> Unto this Darkness which is beyond Light we pray that we may come, and through loss of sight and knowledge may see and know That Which transcends sight and knowledge, by the very fact of not seeing and knowing; for this is real sight and knowledge.[17]

The method of Pseudo-Dionysius was the *via negativa,* or negative theology. If we show by the use of negation our inability to speak of that which is highest, then we also show something of the nature of the highest, or rather, we allow the highest to disclose itself. Negation is like the work of men who carve a statue out of marble. They "remove all the impediments that hinder the clear perception of the latent image and by this mere removal display the hidden statue itself in its hidden beauty."[18] Certainly the way of affirmation and the way of negation, both used by Pseudo-Dionysius, are related. Both are concerned to speak not so much of God in himself, which is the unspeakable thing, but of how it is that man is related to God. Wherever it is possible to say that there is kinship between man and God—and the whole Platonist tradition gives grounds for such a kinship—then the *via analogia* is appropriate. In the *via negativa* "we must start by applying our negations to those qualities which differ from the ultimate goal. Surely it is truer to affirm that God is life and goodness than that He is air or stone, and truer to deny that drunkenness or fury can be attributed to Him than to deny that we may apply to Him the categories of human thought."[19]

The difficulty of negative theology is that it can push beyond thought altogether. Pseudo-Dionysius lists some of the things that God is *not:* He is not soul or mind, not number, and therefore not greatness or smallness. He is not immovable and not in motion. He is not kingship or wisdom, not goodness, not darkness and not light, not error, and not truth. No affirmation or negation, he says, applies to God.[20]

The trouble here is that seemingly *everything* that is "thinkable" at all is denied to God, and the mystics often followed this nihilistic course. A more limited use of negation is developed in St. Thomas, who by a use of analogy is able to say *in what respects* a predicate is to be denied God.

Negative theology is a way of indicating that something is wrong with our best efforts to think "God." Perhaps it is the Neoplatonist counterpart of prophetic judgment; both are critics of man's best efforts. While negative theology can, unfortunately, annihilate God altogether by making him unthinkable, it does have a positive contribution and arises out of the necessary concern of all religion with the contrast between what is "above" and what is "below." The apprehension of holiness does not come without the supposition that symbols drawn from "this world" are unholy representations of "that world." Consciousness of their defect is humility and honesty. Compulsive insistence on their purity is fanaticism. An effort to purify them is reform.

Drawing on the several sources we have been describing, the Medieval mystics, when they entertained the question of man's place in the world, always answered by pointing to a ladder of ascent. Dante could not describe the condition of man in the world without thinking of an upward pilgrimage through the terraces of hell, earth, and heaven. St. Bernard of Clairvaux in *On the Love of God,* described the gradations of love according to the motive of each kind of love. Love of the self for the sake of the self should give way to the next rung, the love of God for the sake of what he gives the self. But the best loves are without self-interest: the love of God for his own sake and, finally, the love of self for God's sake.

The Ascent of Mount Carmel by St. John of the Cross is a work by one who might be called a theorist of practical mysticism, the mysticism of devotion. In that work St. John gives instruction in making a contemplative ascent. To enter upon it the senses must be darkened in a "dark night of the soul." Ultimately, God then grants to the soul "the favor of attaining to being deiform and united in the Most Holy Trinity."[21] St. John of the Cross is the thinker of most immediate influence upon St. Teresa, whom we consider in the next chapter as an example of practical mysticism.

Among the sources of the idea of ascent is, as we have seen, Platonism, with its doctrine of the two realms—the spiritual, real world that is above and the sensible, distorted world here below. The Neoplatonist tradition provided its vision of effulgent light emanating from the One and a vision of the heliotropic soul, gilded in the light, responding and returning to its source. To a great extent, Platonism filtered into the medieval mind by way of Augustine, who furthered and refashioned Platonist dualism by his own philosophical creativity. Like the later thirteenth-century Franciscan Bonaventure, Augustine assumed (as did Platonism, generally) that the thought process itself was hierarchical. By the process of thinking, the mind is lofted by its own logic to a plane where its logic is transcended by the light of God breaking into the mind and completing its thinking for it. A philosophical disposition, even a rationalism, and mysticism are, therefore, by no means necessarily opposed. Certainly, in the mind of the medieval thinker they are not opposed, because one way to enter upon the mystic's pathway is to become a *thinker,* even though, at the end, discursive thought is transcended. We should observe, said Augustine, that there are some things that simply *are* (like stones), some that *know they are* (have intelligence), and some that *know they know,* which is to say, have access to a spiritual and incorporeal realm.[22] The ascent depicted by St. Bonaventure is an *Itinerary of the Mind to God.* The sensual part of the soul can attend to external things and see "footprints" of God upon the world's surface; the intellectual or spiritual part of the soul can look inward and see in itself the "image" of God; and then finally, the mind or apex of the soul can look beyond and above the First Principle of all and gaze in adoration, a vision that transcends intellection but which arises from it.

In the next chapter, concerned with Meister Eckhart and St. Teresa, we examine mysticism of the speculative type, for which the mystic's quest is that of a thinker, and mysticism of the practical type, for which the ascent is progress in prayer and devotion. These distinctions, however, are not rigid. Much thought goes into devotion, and much devotion goes into thought. And if there is an ascent of either kind, there is an implied *continuity*—an unbroken route or pathway—and an implied *discontinuity*—a vision that interrupts the journey, halts the efforts of the wayfarer, and bestows on him, by an act of grace, that which all along he has sought by his own efforts.

Chapter 4
Meister Eckhart
and St. Teresa

Once there was a scholar, devoted to the study of mathematics, who was sitting at his hearth feeling the warm glow of the embers as he concentrated his attention on making some calculations. Suddenly, an intruder burst in. Brandishing a sword, the intruder demanded to know the scholar's name. "Tell me your name. . . . Or I'll kill you!" So absorbed was the scholar in his art that he did not even hear the intruder, who shouted at him for some time until, in a fury, he cut off the scholar's head.

So began the story that Meister Eckhart told as a homily on the spiritual life. The scholar's concentration was due to a purely secular pursuit, mathematics. "How incomparably much more," Eckhart sermonized, "we ought to be absorbed away from things and focus all our faculties on the contemplation, the knowing of the unique, immeasurable, uncreated eternal truth!" To do so, "you must drop all activities and achieve unself-consciousness, in which you will find it."[1]

Both Meister Eckhart and St. Teresa are directed toward a that-worldly aim, but they differ in their approach, their style, and their interests. Eckhart is a mystic of the speculative type. He asked, how can the mind formulate that toward which the mystic aims?

What concepts will serve to point to that which ever recedes beyond concepts altogether? How can the mind think *God*? He clothed the philosophy of Plotinus in the colors of Christian devotion. St. Teresa represents mysticism of a practical type. The word "practical" here does not mean that she occupied herself wholly with good works and this-worldly interests. These played an important part in her life, but the word "practical" primarily means that her teaching derived from her own experience. She tried to say what she herself had found to be true. Her question was not how to *think* God, but how to *approach* God. In a broad sense, all mystics are practical, even the speculative ones. All have a personal, passionate, and operative engagement with their subject, God. Speculative mysticism gives more thought to the nature of that which is approached. Practical mysticism gives more thought to the way of approaching.

Meister Eckhart (1260–1327)

The disposition to probe theoretical questions makes Meister Eckhart the preeminent example of mysticism of the speculative type. His doctrine, rather than his life and example, is what is important. The resources of his thought are largely the Platonist-Aristotelian tradition that he inherited through Augustine, Aquinas, and Pseudo-Dionysius. His feelings and experiences hardly enter into his discourses except where they provide illustrative material for abstract thought. He did have a kind of genius for converting the theoretical into homely examples. He was an effective preacher, one of the first theorists to translate the abstractions of philosophy in the Latin and Greek language to the peoples' language, German. His coined phrases are in fact still useful. Words like "isness" (*istigkeit*), "soul spark" (or "ground of the soul"), and "now-moment" are found to recur frequently in the language of existential theologians.

As a young man, Eckhart entered a Dominican monastery and later studied at Cologne, where Albert the Great, Aquinas's teacher, had taught. He became prior of

Erfurt and vicar of Thuringia and studied at Paris where he received a licentiate and master's degree. Thereafter, he became known as "Meister" Eckhart. He rose in rank to assume various ecclesiastical offices that required considerable managerial skill. His duties required that he travel extensively and preach widely. Because of the trenchant language of his sermons and the unguarded way in which he spoke his subtle thoughts, his doctrine aroused the suspicion of the authorities, and he was posthumously charged with heresy for teachings that "incited ignorant and undisciplined people to wild and dangerous excesses."[2]

Almost the whole of Eckhart's doctrine could be described as his idea of God and his idea of the soul that the idea of God implies.

Eckhart's Doctrine of God. Eckhart's whole doctrine of God is meant to say, with such words as he can devise, that God, as One, is beyond the distinction of words. The words he devises, therefore, are necessarily paradoxical. They have a deliberate shock effect, not unlike the koan of Zen. If he can show a field strewn with shattered words, perhaps his hearers will sense that transcendence was present there. "If anyone imagines that he knows God and his knowledge takes form, then he may know something but it is not God!" God, Eckhart says, in words almost identical to the Hindu conception, is "neither this nor that." Thus, "God is not being . . . he is above being." But in saying this, he cautions, "I have not denied him being but, rather, I have dignified and exalted being in him."[3]

One word-shock is a special consequence of Pseudo-Dionysian thought-forms: the word "goodness" is inapplicable to God. "Goodness" is a word that distinguishes one thing from another and is an inappropriate term for the One, which has no distinctions. It is true that the soul *thinks* of God as good and loves God under "the veil of goodness," but the "intelligence draws aside the veil" and perceives God naked, stripped of goodness or of being or of any name.[4] The intelligence, being superior to the will, is not content to have God hide under the veil of goodness. Here we see the reason that the mystic is, ultimately, more interested in knowing than in doing and deciding. Knowing can transcend itself, but doing and deciding always involve distinguishing some good from some evil. Making any distinction, even ethical ones, falls short of the mystic's vision of the One as an undifferentiated unity.

In addressing the question "What must be true of God if God is, above all, transcendent?" the answers Eckhart came up with were largely directed by the Neoplatonist frame of reference within which he worked. God is not good in any ordinary sense because he is beyond all distinctions of goodness. God is beyond being; he is Being itself or Godhead. The further and perhaps most damaging Platonist assumption was that God must be beyond change. Unfortunately, this idea also often included the unbiblical view that God must not care for man but must be beyond and above being affected by anything less than himself.

> Bear in mind also that God has been immovably disinterested from the beginning and still is and that his creation of the heavens and the earth affected him as little as if he had not made a single creature. . . . All prayers a man may offer and the good works he may do will affect the disinterested God as little as if there were neither prayers nor works, nor will God be any more compassionate or stoop down to man any more because of his prayers and works than if they were omitted.[5]

In adopting the Platonist standard, changelessness, Eckhart also fell heir to a deterministic doctrine. He held that God does not change and, further, that as a perfectly self-consistent being, God *cannot* change. He thereby sacrificed much too much of the personalness of God and bound him to a deterministic schema in which a change of heart and will seemed unthinkable.

> Do not imagine that God is like a carpenter who works or not, just as he pleases, suiting his own convenience. . . .

> When he finds you ready he must act, and pour into you,
> just as when the air is clear and pure the sun must pour
> into it and may not hold back.[6]

Partly responsible for this determinism is Eckhart's penchant for analogies drawn from the natural world. In grasping at ways to speak of God at all, Eckhart, like many mystics, often compares the activity of God to fire and heat or to the rays of the sun or to water being poured from one vessel into another. The activity of God then seems less an operation of a free will than a necessary actualization of potential force. God is a fullness, and if the soul empties itself of creatures, God will automatically fill the void.[7] He *cannot* restrain a process essential to his own nature. Ideas like these were too trying for the Inquisition. In his defense before it, Eckhart cited as his authority an instructive passage from Pseudo-Dionysius' *On the Divine Names:* God is like the sun, and "our sun, through no choice or deliberation, but by the fact of its existence, gives light to all those things which have any inherent power of sharing its illumination."[8] The incident demonstrates how easily metaphors drawn from nature lead to determinism. In the rigor of thinking of God as transcendent, the personal God quite simply disappeared.

Eckhart's Doctrine of the Soul and Its Relationship with God. The spatial analogies Eckhart used disposed him to think of the soul as either entirely filled with God or entirely filled with "creatures." There must be withdrawal or emptying of the soul to make room for God. "To the extent that you eliminate self from your activities, God comes into them—but not more and no less." Largely this either-or choice is introduced by an overly vivid picturing of the soul as a vessel that, in order to be full of God, must be empty of creatures. "No cask holds two kinds of drink at the same time. If the cask is to hold wine, its water must first be poured out, leaving the cask empty and clean. If you are to have divine joy, all your creatures must first be poured out or thrown out."

"Keep this in mind: to be full of things is to be empty of God, while to be empty of things is to be full of God."[9]

Asceticism seems to be the ever-present companion of mysticism. Some withdrawal from "this world" is necessary to make room for "that world." Eckhart's asceticism, however, had nothing to do with self-flagellation or hair shirts. These morbid disciplines did come into the lives of his followers, Suso and Tauler. He himself seemed more interested in the discipline the mind must undergo if it is to think *God*. The part of the self—the creaturely part—that presents an obstacle to God must be removed; then God is united (becomes identical in fact) with the higher part, the soul's spark. "Where the creature ends, there God begins to be. God asks only that you get out of his way, in so far as you are creature, and let him be God in you. . . . The moment you get [one of your own] ideas, God fades out and the Godhead too. It is when the idea is gone that God gets in."[10] Once the soul is rid of creatures it is as fully divine as God himself. After an initial pessimism, which sees the soul filled with creatures, there is an ultimate optimism, which sees the soul united, identical in fact, with God. The mystics do seem to live in the extremes of either utter darkness or incandescent light, but Eckhart expressed the extremes in terms of knowing and unknowing and not in terms of despair and ecstatic joy.

The identity of the soul and God is fostered by two metaphors that are special with Eckhart. One is the idea of the inner kernel or "spark" of the soul that is indistinguishable from God himself.[11] This inner core of the soul, like God, cannot be described. Whatever it is called cannot succeed in naming it because "it [the spark] is neither this nor that"; it is "free of all names and unconscious of any kind of forms." Like God, this interior "soul spark" is a perfect unity "so that there is no possible way to spy it out."[12] Another of Eckhart's metaphors— and a strange one, unique with him—was the figure of birth and begetting. The Eternal Father "begets" his son—not at some time or place but eternally. If one asks

where the begetting and the birth take place, the answer
one receives is that the where and when are hardly
meaningful questions. "Where is he that is born King of
the Jews?" Eckhart's answer shows that the reply could
as well be "In the soul," "In Eternity," or "In God"—
because in God there is no "different" or "differently."[13]
One cannot really distinguish the soul and God.

Eckhart is perhaps the most famous of the mystics for
making the ultimate relationship between the soul and
God so close as to be identical. "God's is-ness (*istigkeit*)
is my is-ness." The soul comes so close to God "that all
the angels . . . shall not see any difference." The soul is
"nearer to God than it is to the body . . . more intimate
with him than a drop of water put into a vat of wine, for
that would still be water and wine; but here, one is
changed into the other so that no creature could ever
again detect a difference between them." "Why did God
become man? So that I might be born to be God—yes—
identically God."[14]

This "deification" of the soul does not take place by
taking thought. And it does not take place in the past or
in the future. One does not remember it or make plans
for it and achieve it; it takes place in what Eckhart and
recent existentialists call the "Now-moment," the "present." The soul needs to be detached from ideas, "free
and empty of them in this Now-moment, the present."
This is to be "a virgin in reality, as exempt from
idea-handicaps as I was before I was born."[15] The end of
the mystic's quest is the recovery of a primordial
innocence, effortlessness, and immediacy.

Reason and Ethics in Eckhart. When it comes to the
classic questions of how man is to know and what man
ought to do, Eckhart is still guided by his vision of God as
an undifferentiated one. It cannot be right, finally, to
make rational or ethical distinctions because, finally, the
distinctions are unreal.

The origin of ideas, Eckhart assumes, (with St.
Thomas and Aristotle), are "outside through the senses."
This is why the soul "can neither conceive nor admit any

idea of itself." It has "no self-knowledge." It is free of all instrumentalities, ideas; and this is why God can unite with it because he too is pure and without ideas or likeness. Thus, the more you can withdraw the "agents of your soul" and forget ideas and things, the nearer you are to God.[16]

> If you are to know God divinely, your own knowledge must become as pure ignorance, in which you forget yourself and every other creature.
>
> But perhaps you will say: "Alas, sir, what is the point of my mind existing if it is to be quite empty and without function? Is it best for me to screw up my courage to this unknown knowledge which cannot really be anything at all? For if I know anything in any way, I shall not be ignorant, nor would I be either empty or innocent. Is it my place to be in darkness?"
>
> Yes, truly. You could do not better than to go where it is dark, that is, unconsciousness.[17]

Such a pessimistic outcome is not the last word. Eckhart holds that the hiddenness, the essential mysteriousness of God, is a great blessing, since it induces wonder and yearning for God. When a person knows the cause of a thing, he soon grows tired of it. "Only this unknown knowledge keeps the soul steadfast and yet ever on the search." There is a preliminary distance between man and God so that man yearns to bridge the gap. "Essence alone satisfies and God keeps on withdrawing farther and farther away, to arouse the mind's zeal and lure it on to follow and finally grasp the true good that has no cause. Thus contented with nothing, the mind clamors for the highest good of all." The intellect "is no more content with [the idea of] God than it would be with a stone or a tree. It can never rest until it gets to the core of the matter, crashing through to that which is beyond the idea of God and truth until it reaches *in principio,* the beginning of beginnings, the source of all goodness and truth."[18]

What, then, can be man's ethical aim? Preliminarily,

it is to "clamor for the highest good of all." Ultimately, it is aimlessness, detachment, or disinterest (*Abgescheidenheit*), or perhaps better, innocence. At times, Eckhart lapses into outright pantheism and speaks of disinterestedness as if it were a mistake to make any distinctions of value at all. When human experience is seen in the light of God, whatever is experienced becomes divine: "shame becomes honor, bitterness becomes sweet, and gross darkness, clear light." "A flea, to the extent that it is in God, ranks above the highest angel in his own right."[19]

Eckhart is pessimistic about moral effort. "I say, categorically, that all the good deeds anyone ever did or might do, together with the time used in doing them, are both lost, time and deeds, all together. . . . A deed is nothing in itself." It knows nothing and therefore is not good or bad. Bad and good are lost together for they "have no duration. . . . God needs them not at all. . . . Therefore, the deed itself is neither good, nor sacred, nor blessed, but rather, he is blessed in whom the fruit of good deeds remains . . . as the capacity to do good, which belongs always to the spirit. For the spirit is in the doing of good and is the good itself."[20]

What is important here is not particular deeds themselves but the total disposition toward the good. This does not end when the deed itself is finished. What is wrong with deeds is that they come to an end. Such goodness as deeds do have is not as good as that condition of the soul that becomes a permanent wellspring of further goodness. Deeds are like time—only momentary, nothing in themselves. Eckhart typically chooses radical expression, but what he says here does not contravene the apostle Paul, who expressed similar ideas in different words: Faith, that more or less permanent interior disposition, is prior to good works. Works flow out of faith; faith is not an achievement built up by works.

It is exactly here, in just such a conception, that mysticism can make a contribution to institutional reform. It can freely set itself against an institutional status quo because externals, for the mystic, are never the final value. Mysticism cannot attach itself to deeds directly and therefore is often ineffective on a purely this-worldly managerial level. Nevertheless, precisely *because* it does not attach itself to particular externals, it can be free to discard them. Its contribution to reform comes not in a practical program it sponsors but in a temper of mind that legitimizes questioning the status quo. It is here that the Protestant Reformation could appropriate something from the tradition of mysticism.[21] With the encouragement of the mystical temper of mind, the institutional forms of religious life can become devalued in the interests of an interior personalism and ethical "disinterestedness." "True possession of God," said Eckhart, does not depend on following a certain method of contemplation but "on the heart and an inner, intellectual return to God." When a person has a true spiritual experience "he may boldly drop external disciplines, even those to which he is bound by vows, from which even a bishop may not release him."[22]

> Do all you do, acting from the core of your soul, without a single "Why." . . . if you imagine that you are going to get more out of God by means of religious offices and devotions, in sweet retreats and solitary orisons, than you might by the fireplace or in a stable, then you might just as well think you could seize God and wrap a mantle around his head and stick him under the table! . . .
>
> Some good people "are hindered by being outwardly too zealous for the blessed sacrament of our Lord's body. . . . Do not cling to the symbols, but get to the inner truth!" . . . We ought to pray not only in temples or on the mountains, but to pray without ceasing everywhere and at all times.[23]

Eckhart and Tillich. One of Eckhart's perplexities as he tried to think *God,* was much like a problem addressed by Paul Tillich. The word or name "God" seems too much to suggest a separate entity, a something or a someone that can be singled out of the undifferentiated unity and then treated as a thing apart. While Eckhart is not consistent in his usage, he usually reserved the word "Godhead" to mean very much what Tillich, in *The Courage To Be*, called the "God above the God of theism." Both Eckhart and Tillich, separated though they are by seven hundred years, are sensitive to the same question. The word "God" is itself too limited in conception to convey that which is ultimate. Too easily, the name conveys the impression of "a being beside others," to use Tillich's phrase. If God is *a* being instead of Being Itself or Godhead, then such a god is subject to the scrutinizing investigations of man and becomes an "object for us as subjects." The ultimate source of absolute faith, or "the courage to be," Tillich calls the "God above the God of theism"—the acceptance of which "makes us a part of that which is not also a part but is the ground of the whole."[24]

There is no question but what Eckhart's distinction between the *Godhead* and *God* (or god) is motivated by the same concern to avoid reifying God. One technique is to say no to conceptions of God marred by finitude. Eckhart, like Tillich, rejected God as an entity.

> God, in so far as he is only god, is not the highest goal of creation. . . . If a flea could have the intelligence to search the eternal abyss of divine being, out of which it came, we should say that god, together with all that god is, could not give satisfaction to the flea! Therefore, we pray that we may be rid of god, and taking the truth break into eternity, where the highest angels and souls too, are like what I was in my primal existence, when I wanted what I was, and was what I wanted.[25]

To minds like Eckhart's and Tillich's with a passion for the "ultimate," some form of negation—some form of atheism—is justifiable if what the atheist would be "rid" of is a god that is too small, a god as "a being," not Being Itself or Godhead. It was Eckhart's passion for the transcendence of God, his refusal to settle for anything short of "ultimate concern," that pressed him into adopting language so prone to misunderstanding and so open to controversy.

Concluding Reflections on Eckhart: The Mystical and the Personal. Eckhart, drawing on the sources at hand—Neoplatonism largely—committed himself to the idea that God is One, and this notion of *Oneness* becomes oversimplified. If, in thinking *One*, the figure of a circle comes to mind, then one sees a circumference, a boundary which marks off an excluded area outside and an included area inside. Where is man's place when one thinks of God like this? Is man an insider or an outsider? Here is where the personal becomes a problem for speculative mysticism. In inheriting the circle, the speculative mystics also inherit an all or nothing view of man.[26] Man is either totally excluded from God by virtue of his creatureliness or totally enfolded within God by virtue of his divine interior "spark." He is like a vessel, either full of God or empty of God, and if empty of God then full of creatures. But which is the real man—the spark or the creature? Is his humanity exalted because there lies within everyone "an aristocrat," a piece of divinity, so that the value of a man is identical to that of God? Or is his humanity brought low because it lies, really, outside in the husk of creatureliness and not inside in the kernel of divinity? What is the essence of man—the kernel or the husk?

Just this ambiguity is mysticism's defect from the standpoint of later theological conceptions of the personal. Man cannot know where he stands. His relationship with God is often viewed in an essentially nonpersonal, geometric pattern. When man is within the circle and identical to God, he must exclude from his attention whatever is outside the circle. He must be as detached and disinterested as is God himself: "For the soul to compare with the abstract spirit of God she must be free from the smallest trace of sensible affection and quite without attachment to anything not God."[27] It was just this tendency to mishandle personal relationships, especially the relationship between man and God, that motivated the criticisms of the modern interpreters of mysticism, whom we consider in later chapters.

Thinking of mysticism as a type of philosophy that has a certain pattern, how are we to place Meister Eckhart within its design.

When one considers God as an undifferentiated unity, what can be said of him? As a *preliminary*, Eckhart says a great deal. He analyzes, he gives examples, he writes sermons, he exhorts. He speaks at great length about what cannot (ultimately) be spoken at all. In all this busy activity with words, he is in accord with the preliminary active phase of the mystic's program. In all this, however, he is a speculative mystic, not a practical one. He is a man of words and thought, and the asceticism he sponsors is more a curtailment of concepts than a curbing of will and desire.

Ultimately, nothing can be said because all words are divisive. A word like "goodness" puts down a boundary against evil. The goodness of God must not exclude anything at all. Therefore, with respect to this world's small goodness, God the One cannot be called good at all. Nor can anyone who still makes ethical or logical distinctions be reunited with this One. Ultimate union with God as One is the recovery of innocence. In a primordial state there could be no restlessness, no agonizing about what is good and what evil, no desire for God or for the truth. There is no separation of any kind. Divinity is "begotten" in the soul, which then recovers the dreaming innocence (the *unwissen,* "unconsciousness") of the prenatal state. From the standpoint of such a state, it is not even true that one "has" a god because there is no separation in terms of which one can "have" anything.

Back in the Womb from which I came, I had no god and merely was, myself. I did not will or desire any truth. Then I wanted myself and nothing else. And what I wanted, I was and what I was, I wanted, and thus, I existed untrammeled by god or anything else. But when I parted from my free will and received my created being, then I had a god. For before there were creatures, God was not god, but rather, he was what he was. When creatures came to be and took on creaturely being, then God was no longer God as he is in himself, but god as he is with creatures.[28]

St. Teresa of Avila (1515–1582)

No doubt St. Teresa is the best known of all Christian mystics. The Catholic tradition, by and large, has adopted her experience with prayer as a kind of standard of excellence for those endowed with the "special gift" of mystical prayer. But more than that, St. Teresa is a personality eminently worth knowing, and her way of writing serves well to introduce her. Even the least mystically inclined reader finds himself meeting an engaging personality and a refreshingly independent mind. "It is a long time since I wrote the last chapter," she wrote one day, and "without reading through what I have written, I cannot remember what I said. However, I must not spend too much time at this, so it will be best if I go right on without troubling about the connection."[29] How freely the mystic sweeps away the nonessentials!

St. Teresa was born in 1515 in the Spanish city Avila, where at twenty-one she became a nun of the Carmelite Convent of the Incarnation. Eventually, troubled by the laxity of her order, she felt a call to restore it to its "primitive" (i.e., original thirteenth-century) strict rule. She set to work to found a convent especially dedicated to the stricter observance, and in 1562 she established the Convent of St. Joseph for reformed ("discalced," or "shoeless") Carmelite nuns.

In these reform efforts, she was an unusually effective diplomat, shrewd enough to avoid open hostility to her project and courageous enough to stick by her convictions. She thought the new convent should embrace the rule of poverty in its purest form and refuse, therefore, to accept a monetary endowment. Not many seemed to agree with her, and her correspondence with the "learned men" who tried to disuade her reveals her tenacity of spirit. It shows that the mystic who consults an interior authority can the more easily set aside external, official authorities.

> I could not persuade myself to allow an endowment. And though they did persuade me now and then that they were right, yet, when I returned to my prayer, and saw Christ on the cross, so poor and destitute, I could not bear to be rich, and I implored Him with tears so to order matters that I might be as poor as He was.[30]

Nor was she above sending off a hot letter to one dissuader who had sent "two sheets by way of reply, full of objections and theology" against her plan. "I answered that, in order to escape from my vocation, the vow of poverty I had made, and the perfect observance of the counsels of Christ, I did not want any theology to help me, and in this case I should not thank him for his learning."[31]

Among the main works of St. Teresa is her *Life*, which interweaves autobiographical facts of an external sort with a painfully honest account of her interior spiritual journey. Her purpose is to teach, not to memorialize; but her teaching is accomplished by indirection. Her readers are to learn by overhearing something of her own struggles and experiences. Her perplexities and problems are as much a part of the message as are her assurances. In her *Life*, she compares the four stages of prayer to four ways of watering a garden. The best way for a garden to be watered is for rain to fall. In the same way, the best manner of prayer is effortless. Later, in *The Interior Castle*, she changed the metaphor to a castle with many mansions *(moradas)* clustered about. The highest form of prayer was like the private, interior mansion, where "the most secret things pass between God and the soul."[32] Another work, *The Way of Perfection*, is addressed to nuns and is straightforward instruction by a mother superior on community and contemplative life.

The thing of arresting interest in the personality of St.

Teresa is her most honest effort to be self-critical. She had no pretense of setting herself up as an authority on mystical theology. Her reason for writing is first of all to be obedient to her superiors, who required her to write "to inspire souls with a longing after so high a good. . . . I will speak nothing that I do not know by great experience." Her aim is practical and experiential. It is not, like Eckhart's, instruction in how to think of God; it is practical advice on how to draw near to God in prayer. Since her message is what she herself has lived through, she includes her doubts within it. She seems to wonder out loud: Does the message have the worth that the writing of it seems to imply? "While I am writing this I may say with St. Paul, 'It is not I who live now; but thou, my Creator livest in me.' . . . Still, I may easily deceive myself, and it may be that I am not what I say I am; but Thou knowest, O my Lord, that to the best of my knowledge, I lie not."[33]

In her *Life*, Teresa describes with warm affection her parents and her brothers and sisters—a well-to-do family of Avila—and she describes herself with self-deprecating amusement that occasionally reverts to self-abasement.

> We were three sisters and nine brothers: all of us, by God's grace, like our parents in virtue, I myself excepted, though I was my father's favourite, and before I began to offend God I think I had some reason to be; for I grieve, when I remember the good inclinations which the Lord had given me, and how badly I made use of them. And my brothers and sisters in no way hindered me from serving God.[34]

She recalled reading the lives of the saints with one of her favorite brothers and the intensity of her childish religious fervor. "It impressed us greatly when we read that the pain and the glory [of the martyrs] was forever. Again and again we talked of this, and we liked to repeat many times 'for ever-ever-ever.'" She wished to die like the martyrs, she said, confessing her childish spiritual folly, "not for any love that I bore [Christ] but to bring

without delay the great riches in Heaven which I read
of. . . . It fills me with devotion even now to think how
early God gave me what I forfeited by my own fault."[35]

Ambitious for martyrdom, Teresa and her brother
made some heroic plans. "We decided to go to the
country of the Moors, begging our way 'for the love of
God,' and to be beheaded there. And I think the Lord had
given us courage enough even at so tender an age, if we
had seen any way of accomplishing this." Naturally
enough, the parents of the children presented, as she
said, "the greatest obstacle to the plan."[36] The children,
who were seven and eleven years old at the time, were
rescued from this escapade by an uncle who found them
crossing a bridge. He returned them to their parents,
who had already begun a search through Avila.

Frustrated in their lofty spiritual ambition, the children turned to the world of imagination and play. "We set
about becoming hermits, and in a garden which we had
at home we contrived to build hermitages as best we
could by piling up small stones which soon fell down;
and so we found no way of satisfying our wishes. . . .
When I played with other little girls I loved to build
convents and play at being nuns; and I think I wanted to
be one, though less so than . . . other things I have
mentioned."[37]

Bathed in such religiosity, Teresa grew up drawing on
the vocabulary, practice, and symbolism of Spanish
Catholicism as she lived through the physical and
spiritual crises that came her way.

> I remember when my mother died I was about twelve years
> old or a little less. When I began to realise my loss I went in
> my grief to an image of Our Lady, and I begged her with
> many tears to take my mother's place. I think that,
> although I did it in my simplicity, it has stood me in good
> stead; for I have found the Virgin by experience to be my
> Sovereign indeed whenever I have recommended myself to
> her, and at last she has brought me back to herself. It
> distresses me now to see and reflect on that which has

prevented me from being faithful to the good desires in
which I began.[38]

Her Practical Life. St. Teresa was well acquainted
with the problems any administrator or headmistress
might face. Her *Way of Perfection,* written as a practical
aid to nuns, especially reflects her common sense and
psychological insight, as well as her outright disdain for
misguided confessors. If a nun's confessor tends toward
vanity, she advised, a nun should view his opinions with
suspicion and make her confession short. In fact, she
would be well advised to tell her superior that she "does
not get on with him and go elsewhere." St. Teresa
consistently warned against the misjudgments of confessors and spiritual directors who, she said, could
sometimes simply "be silly"[39] and make a nun feel that it
is better to obey him than her superior. She felt free to
judge the value of the spiritual direction she received.
She trusted her own judgment and had a thoroughly
independent mind.

Her psychological insights show a great degree of
realism. She has this to say about the administrative
problems of a prioress managing her nuns:

> She sees you wailing about a mere nothing as if your heart
> were breaking. . . . Sometimes the Poor Prioress sees that
> your request is excessive, but what can she do? She feels a
> scruple if she thinks she has been lacking in charity and
> she would rather the fault were yours than hers: she
> thinks, too, that it would be unjust of her to judge you
> harshly.[40]

Once a very rich lady was so deep in grief over the
death of her husband that she seemed beyond consolation. Having heard of Teresa, she conceived the notion
that she, perhaps, could offer some consolation. Since
the lady was of considerable influence, she was able to
persuade the provincial to require Teresa, along with a
companion, to come stay with her for a time. The whole
episode provides a fascinating glimpse into the reactions

of a contemplative suddenly thrown into the self-indulgent life of a wealthy Spanish lady.

Her experience there, she says, "was as it were a cross for me; for the comforts of her house were a great torment, and her making so much of me made me afraid."

> I saw that she was a woman, and as much liable to passion and weakness as I was; that rank is of little worth, and the higher it is, the greater the anxiety and trouble it brings. People must be careful of the dignity of their state, which will not suffer them to live at ease; they must eat at fixed hours and by rule, for everything must be according to their state, and not according to their constitutions; and they have frequently to take food fitted more for their state than for their liking.
>
> God deliver me from this wicked artificial life!—though I believe that this lady, not withstanding that she was one of the chief personages of the realm, was a woman of great simplicity, and that few were more humble than she was. I was sorry for her, for I saw how often she had to submit to much that was disagreeable to her, because of the requirements of her rank. Then, as to servants, though this lady had very good servants, how slight is that little trust that may be put in them! One must not be conversed with more than another; otherwise, he who is so favoured is envied by the rest. This of itself is a slavery, and one of the lies of the world is that it calls such persons masters, who, in my eyes are nothing else but slaves in a thousand ways.[41]

Stages of Prayer. In listening to St. Teresa's advice on prayer, what needs to be kept in mind is the common assumption on the part of the mystics that there are two general types of prayer. There is a lower, ordinary level of prayer, which involves some effort on the part of the one who prays. He meditates and formulates his prayer in words and is conscious of making a prayerful effort. Then there is a higher level of extraordinary or "supernatural" prayer, for which the efforts of the lower level are only a preparation. This higher form of prayer is given by grace and not won by effort. Nevertheless, it is not possible to spring directly into the upper level of prayer without going through a stage of preparation. Little by little, one works at prayer and finds that the effort gradually gives way so that the final and highest type of prayer is one that is entirely bestowed by God upon man without any effort on his part. This is prayer given purely by grace, or "infused" prayer. The hierarchical schema of Platonism is the background of these stages of prayer.

Progress in prayer, as St. Teresa charmingly describes it, is to be compared to the way one waters a garden. We have to be good gardeners. God, she says, has already rooted up the weeds; we have only to tend and water the garden so that what God has planted will blossom.[42]

The first way to water the garden is "by water taken out of a well, which is very laborious." In this kind of prayer the beginner must work at "keeping the senses recollected" because "the senses have been hitherto accustomed to distractions."[43] The beginner needs to disregard what he sees and hears. He must meditate on the life of Christ until the understanding becomes wearied. This kind of prayer is one in which the understanding, through meditative acts, is at work. St. Teresa seems to regard this as a self-help type of prayer—though accompanied by grace. At some point, though, the understanding stops its operations because God suspends it.

> For when our Lord suspends the understanding, and makes it cease from its acts, He puts before it that which astonishes and occupies it: so that, without making any reflections, it shall comprehend in a moment more than we could comprehend in many years with all the efforts in the world.[44]

The second way is to draw water from a well by means of buckets and a windlass, a way that is less troublesome and which gives more water. In this context, she begins to describe what she calls the "prayer of quiet," which is the beginning of "contemplative" prayer. In *The Interior Castle,* where the stages of prayer are described in terms of progress from one mansion to another (not, as she says, arranged in a row but clustered like the fronds of a "palmito" surrounding its stalk), this prayer corresponds to the fourth mansion and, as she describes it: "The faculties are stilled and have no wish to move, for any movement they make appears to hinder the soul from loving God." [45] The soul has a desire for rest like one who has almost but not quite completed his journey. The will gives its simple consent to God, but the other faculties— the memory and the understanding, are not as content as the will and "come and go." Generally, the prayer is not wearisome because it is not laborious. While St. Teresa's prayer of quiet appears to be an attitude of rest, it is not yet the culmination of the spiritual quest, and in *The Way of Perfection,* she has a puzzling sentence to the effect that this state of prayer sometimes continues for a day or two so that the active life and the contemplative life are united as one attends to business. "Martha and Mary work together." [46]

The third state of prayer is compared to watering a garden by means of a brook or river. Here there is very much less trouble in watering, "although there is still some in directing the water." There is an increase of grace and a cessation of effort. "To me it seems to be nothing else but a death, as it were, to all the things of this world, and a fruition of God." In this state of prayer, all the faculties are occupied wholly with God, "not one of them ventures to stir." [47] The flowers are opening and beginning to be fragrant.

This "third water" (or, as it is described in *The Interior Castle,* "the fifth mansion") is the "prayer of union" or "perfect" or "true" contemplation, to which the previous steps have been a preparation. St. Teresa's own experience while in this state of prayer she described in her *Life:*

O my King, seeing that I am now, while writing this, still
under the power of this heavenly madness, an effect of Thy
mercy and goodness—and it is a mercy I never
deserved—grant, I beseech Thee, that all those with whom
I may have to converse may become mad through Thy
love, or let me converse with none, or so order it that I may
have nothing to do in the world, or take me away from it.
This Thy servant, O my God, is no longer able to endure
sufferings so great as those are which she must bear when
she sees herself without Thee: if she must live, she seeks
no repose in this life—and do Thou give her none. This my
soul longs to be free—eating is killing it, and sleep is
wearisome; it sees itself wasting the time of this life in
comforts, and that there is no comfort for it now but in
Thee; it seems to be living contrary to nature—for now, it
desires to live not in itself, but in Thee.[48]

The fourth way of watering the garden is by showers of
rain "when Our Lord Himself waters it." This way is
without any labor on the part of the one who prays and is
"incomparably better than all others."[49] In all the other
ways there is some labor still done by the one who prays,
although in the third way, the labor is attended, she says,
by bliss and comfort of the soul. In this fourth state,
"there is no sense of anything, only fruition, without
understanding what that is the fruition of which is
granted. . . . The senses are all occupied in this fruition
in such a way that not one of them is at liberty, so as to
attend to anything else, whether outward or inward."[50]
Breathing and bodily strength fail. The eyes close
involuntarily. If they are open, they see nothing.
Reading, if attempted, is to no avail; the understanding
furnishes no help in it. What is heard is not com-
prehended and it is useless to try to speak. No doubt
what is achieved in this fourth level of prayer is
something like what Eckhart described in his term
unwissen. The step-by-step advance is made and then
discursive reason drops away as the efforts of the will
turn to effortlessness. "The understanding is of no help."

Trances and Visions. The progression that is implied

in St. Teresa's stages of prayer lends itself to intellectualizing—however beyond intellection the outcome may be. The progression is a step-by-step advance and can be described, therefore, in terms of antecedents and outcome. It compares in form with discursive reason. Experiences like trances and visions are quite different. They are sudden intrusions totally without antecedents and therefore are totally irrational. The peculiarity of mysticism is that it sustains both a continuity and the sudden disruption of the continuity.

St. Teresa is, of course, well known as one who experienced trances, although she was not inclined to exult in them or to recommend that prayer be undertaken with an eye to inducing them. Rapture, trance, and mystical union, she explained, have only minor differences. A trance is more visible in its effects and more "violent" in nature. Breathing diminishes, and it is impossible to open the eyes or to speak. The hands become cold and "sometimes stiff and straight as pieces of wood."[51]

One scruple that beset persons like Teresa who had such experiences was the question of their origin. Were the sensations of God or of the devil? Ultimately it was churchly authority that would determine the answer. When Teresa had a vision of Christ "as He is after His resurrection," some she said, suspected her of having had a visitation of the devil and would have had her exorcized.

> On one occasion, when I was holding in my hand the cross of my rosary, He took it from me into His own hand. He returned it; but it was then four large stones incomparably more precious than diamonds; for nothing can be compared with what is supernatural.[52]

Her account of a vision of Satan produces an odd mixture of the fantastic and the practical by offering advice to any who should need to know that throwing holy water at Satan always works well to make him disappear:

> I was once in an oratory, when Satan, in an abominable shape, appeared on my left hand. I looked at his mouth in particular, because he spoke, and it was horrible. A huge flame seemed to issue out of his body, perfectly bright, without any shadow. He spoke and said though I had escaped out of his hands, he would yet lay hold of me again.

She threw holy water at him, and he disappeared.[53]

One of St. Teresa's most famous visions is of an angel with a spear of gold.

> It was our Lord's will that in this vision I should see the angel in this wise. He was not large, but small of stature, and most beautiful—his face burning, as if he were one of the highest angels, who seem to be all of fire. . . .
>
> I saw in his hand a long spear of gold, and at the iron's point there seemed to be a little fire. He appeared to me to be thrusting it at times into my heart, and to pierce my very entrails; when he drew it out, he seemed to draw them out also, and to leave me all on fire with a great love of God. The pain was so great that it made me moan; and yet so surpassing was the sweetness of this excessive pain, that I could not wish to be rid of it. The soul is satisfied now with nothing less than God. The pain is not bodily, but spiritual; though the body has its share in it, even a large one. It is a caressing of love so sweet which now takes place between the soul and God, that I pray God of his goodness to make him experience it who may think that I am lying.[54]

She says this lasted some days, during which she could speak with no one, but only cherish the pain. The scene described by Teresa is vividly depicted in sculpture by the seventeenth-century artist Bernini, in the Cornaro Chapel in Santa Maria della Vittoria. It is the *Ecstasy of St. Teresa.*

Concluding Reflections on St. Teresa: Continuity or Discontinuity? The larger question of the mystic's experience of rapture and trance is not whether his or her experience represents something real—nor is it even its interesting psychological and erotic implications. It is, rather, the question of how the mystics see the relation of nature to supernature. Is there a slow, steady climb out of nature up to God as is implied by the stages of prayer? Or is there a sudden intrusion into nature from divine or demonic regions? The mystical tradition can support either alternative.

No doubt the popular mind is disposed to identify mysticism with visions and trances. Such a view appreciates too little the hierarchical nature of mysticism as a way of thought and concerns itself too much with the mystical as a sudden and irrational experience. It is also possible that the sudden, irrational experience itself can become rationalized if the oddity of the experience is made into a kind of proof or validation of its supernaturalness. This rational sanctioning of oddity can attend both Catholicism and Protestantism. It is evidenced by an exaggerated preference for the miraculous or for the authority of one who is newly and suddenly converted—a twice born rather than a once born. It is possible that the current Pentecostal movement, the Jesus movement, and similar enthusiasms contain within them a yearning for some empirical evidence which suddenness and disruption seem to provide. It is surprising how often the mystics themselves either denounce or have cautionary advice to give on the phenomenon of trances and raptures. Messengers sent to people, as through an angel, "rarely happen and to few people," said Eckhart. "Incomparably better" than these is the "love of God and the intimacy with him which binds man to him."[55] Similar views are expressed by the author of *The Cloud of Unknowing*, St. Catherine of Genoa, and St. John of the Cross. With the exception of William James, and others concerned with the psychology of mysticism, the classic interpreters of mysticism of the turn of the century (to whom we give our attention in the next chapter) interested themselves more in the rational continuity implied by mysticism than in its irrational disruptions.

For this reason, Cuthbert Butler, von Hügel, and Inge do not make the visions of St. Teresa central to their interpretations. While their motive is not to discredit Teresa, they say that interpreting mysticism exclusively in terms of her visionary experiences has given disproportionate weight to strangeness and abnormality as a feature of mysticism.

As we see, St. Teresa's program was, on the surface, not like Eckhart's. She did not set about telling how to think of *Being Itself,* which is to say, how to think of God or Godhead. Her writing and teaching had the practical aim of teaching how to pray. A practical aim cannot be undertaken, however, in the absence of an assumed world view. Her descriptions of the stages of prayer assume that there is an ascent to God; she means to tell about the rungs on the ladder. She assumes, certainly, that there is a two-layer world—a "this world" and a "that world."[56] "This world" must be left behind by an act of self-mortification. Death and dying are words found often in her prayers. Let us practice penance and mortification; let the silk worm die when its work is done. "Then we shall see God and shall ourselves be as completely hidden in his greatness as is this little worm in its cocoon."[57] For all her practicality and this-worldly common sense, Teresa, like Eckhart, assumed that the man-God relationship is either-or: to be filled with God is to be empty of creatures. Her greatness, and the reason she so eminently deserves to be read, is that she speaks of the fullness of God from out of her own experience of it.

Speculative and Practical Mysticism

While it is useful to distinguish between speculative and practical mysticism, the distinction is merely relative and can be overdrawn. The distinction lies not so much in a difference of intellectual presupposition as in a difference of emphasis. How important is abstract thinking itself? To the speculative mystics, forming the right idea of God, the right idea of Being Itself, is a matter of overwhelming importance, and the emotional fervor that attaches to it is an intellectual love of God that vaults the mind to inexpressible reaches of transcendence. While Eckhart often uses colorful, concrete language, he does so in the interest of an ontological idea he means to set forth. In St. Teresa, the imagery itself is, in a sense, the substance of her message. Her focus is experience, not being, and her emotional fervor is a "sweetness," an exquisite "pain," a "caressing of love."

In the East, the distinction between speculative and practical mysticism is represented by Advaita Vedantism and Bhakti. One of the issues in comparative mysticism is the question of whether all mysticism, whether of East or West, is simply the same. If one wished to defend the sameness of all mysticism, the best support would be the speculative mystics. What they have in view most nearly transcends the accidents of race or geography. Thus Rudolf Otto in *Mysticism East and West* was able to give an extended comparison of the Advaita Vedantism of Shankara and the speculative Christian mysticism of Eckhart. What Shankara describes as Brahman and Isvara, Eckhart calls Godhead and God. For both, the Godhead (or Brahman) is incomprehensible and inexpressible, without mode of being. It is the One "before whom words recoil." Where Eckhart speaks of the identity of the soul and God, Shankara speaks of the identity of Brahman and Atman. In this vein, it is possible, especially in the case of the speculative mystics, to excise accidental differences of language in order to expose a common philosophical outlook. Aldous Huxley's *Perennial Philosophy* is the classic example of such a method. In the case of a practical mystic like Teresa, the accidents of time, locale, language, and personal traits of character—far from being irrelevant to the message—are more nearly the substance of it. The tools of history, sociology, psychology, and literature are more applicable to the practical mystics; the tools of philosophy, more applicable to the speculative mystics. Nevertheless, philosophical presuppositions are at work in both; and these, in the case of Eckhart and Teresa, are largely Neoplatonist, disposing them both to a hierarchical pattern of thought.

PART THREE
Interpretations

If it is the destiny of mysticism to lose its life in philosophy, it is the destiny of philosophy to recover its hold upon its object by renewal of the mystic vision.

Reason may establish our certainties; it does not initiate them.

—Charles A. Bennett

Chapter 5
Premises of
Modern Interpretation

St. Bernard of Clairvaux used to gather his monks around him and speak to them of something he himself had experienced—a love of God so pure and so intense that it all but transformed human love into divine love. "Molten, white-hot iron," he said, is as much like fire, as "air when flooded with the sun's pure light" is like the "very light itself." St. Catherine of Genoa would say to her followers, "If of what my heart feels but one drop were to fall into Hell, Hell itself would altogether turn into Eternal Life." And St. Teresa promised her reader: "I will speak nothing that I do not know by great experience."[1] Those who could speak like this had a persuasiveness that lay, not in their logic, but in themselves and their practice. And the ones to whom they spoke listened not merely with the interest of an observer but with the painstaking attention of the apprentice. The one who taught, taught out of his own experience; the one who learned, learned something that he would try to do.

A critical perspective was by no means absent from the mystics, but mysticism among the classic mystics, whether speculative or practical, was a practice. When criticisms were offered, they were for the sake of pointing out rough places in the pathway where the apprentice might stumble. We next focus on critical interpretations of mysticism by the sympathetic outsider. At this transition point, it may be helpful to take a backward glance at what has gone before.

Reconsidering the Sources

By now we have seen enough to realize the confusing array of material that the word "mysticism" calls forth. What is mysticism?

Mysticism is the living out of a world view of a special kind: what meets the eye as man looks out at his world is indicative of something more, higher, or deeper than its mere appearance. Mysticism, whatever the terms used, makes a distinction between a "this world" (the appearance) and a "that world" (the deeper reality). The mystic, however, is not simply a theorist; he is one engaged in living a life based on his world view. In this sense the mystic is often called *practical* by those who interpret him. In everyday language the word "practical" would hardly seem to apply. On the mystic's scale of value the "that world" takes precedence over the "this world," and that is precisely the *impractical* nature of this scale of value as we ordinarily view it. The mystic's practicality means that he intends to *live* his philosophical program. What he thinks he ought to do is to strengthen his relationship with the real (that world). If he has a strongly dualistic view, as is the case with medieval Western mysticism, his program will include lessening his ties with "this world." *Asceticism* is the name of this disengagement, and the *via negativa* is the epistemological application of asceticism. If he has a less dualistic view, as in the case of Zen or Taoism, his program will aim at "seeing into" the way things are, seeing the deeper reality manifest in the actual appearance. Aesthetic appreciation of appearance (of "this world") and not disengagement from it will be his aim.

What we have called the pattern of mysticism includes a theory about the world and a life lived in accordance with the theory. It has a two-step program. In the *preliminary* stage of the pattern of mysticism, the world seems dualistic. *Ultimately,* the mystic must find a way to make it one. *Preliminarily,* he may be busy and active in his work of training and preparation. *Ultimately,* he is passive, that is, at peace and in harmony with his goal.

The word "mysticism" may become attached to some part of the pattern without reference to the pattern as a whole. If it is attached to the intellectual vision of the world from which the mystic's practice is launched, then it is possible to identify mysticism with Neoplatonism in the West and monistic Vedantism in the East. Or the word may attach to the *method* used to attain a reunion with the mystic's goal, and in the popular mind this is often the usage. "Mysticism" may then mean simply the postures and techniques of meditation and prayer or perhaps mind-over-matter mortification of the flesh. The word may also attach to a certain temperament. "Mystical" may describe a "disinterested" equanimity of mind, the sense of harmony and peace that characterizes the mystic who has attained his aim. The word may attach to that warmer feeling of personal love, the fervor of Bhakti religion and the practical mysticism of the West.

Blindly fingering the many faces of mysticism, several convictions begin to take shape.

1. Mysticism has a preliminary ethical interest, but mysticism is not an ethic. While mystics like St. Teresa and the author of *The Cloud of Unknowing* are found to recommend virtue, they do so as a preparation for some fuller life. Virtue and ethical decisiveness are unneeded once the harmony or unity with the ultimate is reached. Wherever there is an "ought" there is an effort; unity and harmony mean precisely that effort is now unneeded.

What portions of the Bible are mystical are those which have the least ethical decisiveness. In one way of thinking, one of the most "mystical" episodes in the Bible is the parable of the workers in the vineyard, in which those who come early and those who come late receive (unfairly from the this-worldly perspective) the same wage. Meister Eckhart made ethical *disinterestedness* one of the hallmarks of the mystic's life. Taoism represents a view that is "mystical " in that it describes a mysticism already fully realized and unneedful of moral self-assertion: it is without strife, without the need of ethical decisiveness; it is peace, grace, not in the sense of a bestowal from on high, but in the sense of poise and harmony with the world's way of going, the Tao. Wherever there is tension between the ethical and the aesthetic interests, mysticism will be with the aesthetic.

2. Mysticism, when its metaphysical interest is highest, can seem—or at least it is frequently criticized in this respect—empty of personal engagement and passion. God becomes blank, devoid of content. Today, among churchmen, little religious fervor seems to be associated with questions of being. The question of being is seldom asked within the framework of current religious institutions. It is left to science to ask the question of being at the frontier of knowledge. Where science runs out of empirical explanations, it cannot suppress the question of the sources of its empirical data. There, it may also recover something of the mystic's passion for Godhead, or Being Itself. "The most beautiful and most profound emotion we can experience," said Albert Einstein, "is the sensation of the mystical. It is the sower of all true science. He to whom this emotion is a stranger, who can no longer wonder and stand rapt in awe, is as good as dead. To know that what is impenetrable to us really exists, manifesting itself as the highest wisdom and the most radiant beauty which our dull faculties can comprehend only in their most primitive forms—this knowledge, this feeling is at the center of true religiousness."[2] The speculative mystics debated the question of being with religious fervor. They had an existential awareness of being which they thought to celebrate. As celebrants of being, they are the forerunners of contemporary thinkers like Heidegger, Jaspers, Marcel, and Tillich.

3. Certain distortions appear in both a religion of feeling (practical mysticism) and a religion of being

(speculative mysticism) that the study of mysticism makes especially evident. With respect to feeling, the question arises whether the feeling lies inside man or between man and God. If feeling is purely subjective, then God, though seeming most real and most near to feeling, is removed from transcendence and becomes housed inside man himself, thereby exalting man to a divine level. Self-worship of some kind is the end result. Speculative mysticism can remove God by refining him into nonexistence simultaneously as it refines its concept of being by the use of negatives. It can also remove God by making his nature not merely akin to man's nature but identical with it. And, again, some form of self-worship can be the result.

A "relationship" between man and God needs to preserve the distinction between man and God, as well as to allow for a kinship. Much of the mystics' language of paradox was aimed at expressing this tension. Plato's concept of participation, his parable of the cave, and the Zagreus myth had this tension in view. But the mystics' vivid sense of the presence of God, coupled with their uncritical use of spatial analogies, pushed them toward the simple identification of God and man. Christian mysticism, above all, must work toward a relationship, not a merger. The distortions of mysticism forewarn the theologian of the difficulties involved in expressing a personal relationship between man and God.

4. In any assessment of mysticism (or religion generally) as rational or irrational, it is helpful to have in mind a distinction like that made by Plotinus and the mystics. Reason has more than one level and more than one function. The deeper or higher kind of reason, *Nous,* is nondiscursive—a direct, unifying intuition. It is prepared for by *epistēmē* and *dianoia*—discursive "technical reason" (to use Tillich's phrase)—which sorts out the reasons, causes, and effects of events. Certainly, the ultimate aim of mysticism is a rational aim in the sense of *Nous.* In the preliminary, preparatory stage of mysticism—that stage which uses a technique—

mysticism may also be rational in the sense of technical reason. If by habit of mind we will grant the word "rational" only to technical reason, then the ultimate aim of mysticism will be said to be irrational. To the Platonist tradition, however, to transcend a lower level of reason is to be rational still. As we shall see, all three of the modern classic interpreters of mysticism we consider in chapter 6 choose to preserve some rational continuity in mysticism. They object to identifying the mystical with an irrational intrusion into an otherwise rational world. They hold that the mystical apprehension is a deepening of reason itself.

Mysticism in Critical Perspective

At the beginning of the twentieth century there was a renewed interest in the study of mysticism on the part of those who were not mystics themselves. While many of the studies were warmly sympathetic, all were critical in a more detached way than were the classic mystics. In 1901, William James included in his Gifford Lectures, "The Varieties of Religious Experience," a personal disclaimer: "Whether my treatment of mystical states will shed more light or darkness, I do not know, for my own constitution shuts me out from their enjoyment almost entirely, and I can speak of them only at second hand."[3] Whether we are to take James' demurrer entirely seriously has been questioned in the light of his biography. But it is clear that he does not intend to study mystical experience as a mystic himself. From some distance, he expects to take a look at the storehouse of religious sentiments found in individuals and to report on what he finds.

When in 1911 Evelyn Underhill wrote her interpretive classic *Mysticism,* her interest in the subject was strongly devotional. Nevertheless, like James, she kept some critical distance between herself and her subject and spoke in the language of appreciation, not of autobiography. What, she asked, does the story of mysticism "mean for us; for unmystical men?"[4] And her answer is that the mystic's path is a great example of *all men's* spiritual development.

The New Science of Psychology. A number of factors influenced the way in which the early twentieth-century studies of mysticism were undertaken. Of first importance for James and others who wished to use an empirical method was the comparatively new science of psychology. It provided a way of describing "religious consciousness" without committing oneself to the truth of religious doctrine. Description, not doctrine, was the aim. Not metaphysics but experience was the subject of investigation. As James put it:

> In all sad sincerity I think we must conclude that the attempt to demonstrate by purely intellectual processes the truth of the deliverances of direct religious experience is absolutely hopeless. . . If [philosophy] will abandon metaphysics and deduction for criticism and induction, and frankly transform herself from theology into science of religions, she can make herself enormously useful.[5]

A similar point of departure is suggested in the work of the personal idealist James Bissett Pratt (*The Religious Consciousness,* 1920). Like James, Pratt eschews doctrine and defines mysticism as "the consciousness of a Beyond." James Leuba, a psychologist who is unsympathetic to mysticism, wrote *The Psychology of Religious Mysticism* (1925). It is an interpretation of mysticism that speaks in the Freudian terms of *death wish, world flight,* and *sexual repression.* Typically there was no desire on the part of psychological treatments like these to certify the mystics' experience as valid. Pratt said that his purpose was purely descriptive. He means to describe "religious consciousness" without having "any point of view."

The Historical Interest in Mysticism. Another factor in the critical evaluations of mysticism was the historical interest of its interpreters. Whatever can be looked at as if it were past, can be looked at with detachment. It is one thing for St. Bernard to address his monks or for St.

Teresa to explain how to pray. It is another thing for the historian to examine what St. Bernard and St. Teresa were saying and why. More often than not, however, historical studies of mysticism were undertaken with an eye to the spiritual benefit that could be derived from the mystics. What can those who pray learn from those who have recorded their experience with prayer? Evelyn Underhill's concern with mysticism is based on the conviction that mystical experience is not the exclusive province of the specialist, that it is not an esoteric or occult phenomenon, and that it may become a common experience. She concentrated more on the lessons to be learned from practical mysticism than on the philosophical reflections of speculative mysticism. And it is her knowledge of the history of the literature of mysticism that gives her access to its value. Similar in approach is the work of the American Quaker Rufus Jones. His *Studies in Mystical Religion* (1908) is filled with valuable chapters—the ones on Meister Eckhart and Dionysius the Areopagite are especially noteworthy—that recover for the modern reader the perennial value of classic mysticism. Friedrich von Hügel's *Mystical Element of Religion* (first published in 1908), is a philosophical-historical study of mysticism in the light of St. Catherine of Genoa. In every way it is dependent on the tools of the historian and on von Hügel's interest in providing textual criticism of the sources.

Of central importance to the historians of mysticism was their obligation to be critical in order to recover the real values of mysticism. They wished to disengage the best of mysticism from its nonessential accretions like fanaticism, imaginative visions, and ascetic excesses. On the philosophical side, they wished to rid mysticism of exclusive dependence on the negative language that pushed it into nihilism. "True mysticism" had to be distinguished from "false mysticism." Dom Cuthbert Butler's study, *Western Mysticism* (1922), had just this program in view. In his treatment of the mysticism of Augustine, Gregory the Great, and Bernard of Clairvaux,

Butler focuses on the type of mysticism he wishes to name "Western." The adjective is not meant to distinguish it from non-Christian "Eastern" religions. It indicates, rather, the mysticism of the Western, Latin church not yet formed by the Eastern, negative predicates of Pseudo-Dionysius. What Butler tries to recover is not speculative mysticism but a "mysticism purely and solely religious, objective, and empirical; being merely, on the practical side, the endeavour of the soul to mount to God in prayer and seek union with Him and surrender itself wholly to His love; and on the theoretical side, just the endeavour to describe the first-hand experiences of the personal relations between the soul and God in contemplation and union."[6]

The Search for an Essence of Religion. As a third factor in the new critical approach to mysticism, we can name an interest which, in a way, is the logical extension of the historian's interest in the general relevance of mysticism. It is the search for an essence of religion that transcends every time and place. The mystical spirit itself, in its interest in the timeless and spaceless, lends itself to such a characterization. Is there an essence of religion? And can mysticism, which Aldous Huxley called the "perennial philosophy" make a claim to being the essence of religion?

A search for the essence of religion was the natural outcome of the rationalism of the Enlightenment, which led theologians to work toward statements that were universally true and to stop pleading their cause by way of miracle. The truth must be a seamless garment; where does religion (and Christianity in particular) fit in? The search for the contribution of religion—the essence of religion—was undertaken by the disciplines of history of religion, theology, and anthropology. Schleiermacher in the nineteenth century looked for it in the "feeling of absolute dependence"—a somewhat more rational, less emotional disposition than the words seem to imply. The efforts of Schleiermacher were continued by Rudolf Otto, whose work *The Idea of the Holy* (German, 1917;

English, 1924) is indispensable to a study of mysticism. Otto identifies the essential feature of religion as the holy or numinous, a concept derived from ancient Roman religion and one that he describes not in terms of moral goodness but in terms of "creature feeling." In contrast to Schleiermacher's "feeling of absolute dependence," Otto's creature feeling is a *direct* apprehension of one's creaturehood before majesty; it is not a derived rational inference that one has been created or caused. Creature feeling is characterized by *mysterium tremendum,* or the sense of the divine (or God) as "wholly other," Otto's most quoted phrase. Creature feeling is also charac- terized by a *mysterium fascinans,* a sense of kinship with the divine that compels one to draw near. Taken together, the *mysterium fascinans* and the *mysterium tremendum* indicate the double religious experience found in the scripture of the world's religions: the experience of being succored and the experience of being forbidden; the experience of being welcomed and received and the experience of being rejected and shut out; the experience of grace and the experience of sin. Otto succeeded in putting into experiential categories those mystical conceptions that had been expressed in more metaphysical language by such speculative mystics as Pseudo-Dionysius and Eckhart. Otto makes the *via negativa* understandable as a religious experience, not just a metaphysical speculation. Or rather, we should say, the new vocabulary he provides recovers the experiential nature that always lay behind the metaphys- ical language of the speculative mystics.

A part of the discussions about the essence of religion had to do with the advisability of looking for an essence of religion at all. Those who did so—like Schleiermacher, Otto, and the nonmystical, more moralizing theologians Harnack and Ritschl—were concerned to find the meaning of religion in general and of Christianity as one type of religion, albeit the most excellent type. They looked for general truths and thus for the common denominator of the religious life. Mysticism could at least

come under consideration as a possible common denominator. So could moralism, for which the central
issue was the disposition of the will. Among those who
looked for an essence of religion, the question was not
the propriety of the task but what one found the essence
to be. The mystical and the moral vied for the honor of
being named the "essence" of religion.

To the Barthians and neo-orthodox, this search for an
essence, for a universal truth of religion, was wrong at its
inception. The value of Christianity, they held, does not
lie in what can be held as true of it *in general.* It is not
one type of religion distinguished in excellence from
others only in degree. A search for a common denominator of religions will, they feared, end in the total
dissolution of the uniqueness of Christianity, converting
it into a type of religious philosophy resembling Feuerbach's subjectivist humanism.[7] The divine revelation, as
they saw it, is received only by grace and is not a
perception of a superior intellect that, in reliance on
itself, discerns the essence of religion.

The way mysticism was evaluated became inextricably
mixed with this post-Enlightenment search for an
essence of religion and with criticisms of this search. We
can roughly schematize some of the possible positions:

Pro Essence of Religion, Antimystic
Roughly the position of Harnack and Ritschl. While
they agree on the search for an essence of religion,
they are antimystic by virtue of finding the essence
in moral excellence, not in mystical apprehensions.
Influencing their view of mysticism was a Kantian
individualism that spurned mystical engulfment of
the self; and, in the case of Harnack especially, his
Protestant view of mysticism as "Catholic piety."

Pro Essence of Religion, Promystic
The position of Schleiermacher and Otto. Christianity, it is held, is the best type of religion. It answers a
generally felt need on the part of all men. While the
impulse to locate an "essence" of religion is born of a

desire to make religion rational, in the case of Otto, especially, the quest ends with a full appreciation for nonrational and nonmoralistic (mystical?) elements in religious life—the "numinous." The position represented here is in some ways "promystic" and "antimoralistic."

Anti Essence of Religion, Antimystic (and Antimoralistic)

Neo-orthodoxy. The position of Emil Brunner, whom we examine later. When man looks for an essence of religion, he looks with his own discerning eye to his own experience. God becomes an ideal or value that man himself can entertain by taking thought. The result is introspection and self-worship. This is the result whether the essence is interpreted mystically or morally. Neo-orthodoxy thus aligns moralism and mysticism and rejects both with the same gesture by which it rejects any concern with an essence of religion. Both seem to begin egocentrically—with man and his experience—instead of theocentrally—with God and his transcendence.

Catholic Modernism. A fourth factor in the turn-of-the-century interest in mysticism was the doctrinal uncertainty of the times, evidenced especially by the movement called Catholic Modernism. Earlier scientific work on the part of biblical scholars like Wellhausen and Schweitzer had called into question a literal biblical orthodoxy. Intellectual honesty required a critical reading of the Scriptures, a thing that had always been done by such giants as Augustine, Luther, and other great theologians, but which now precipitated a kind of crisis in the hearts of those who felt themselves bound to the institutional pronouncements of the church. How were miracles to be understood? How was Darwin's theory to be reconciled with the Genesis account? Did Jesus have a culturally limited view of the world? Paul expected a speedy eschaton, obviously not fulfilled. Are his sayings and the sayings of Jesus thereby discredited?

In the light of such questions, which seemed so profoundly unsettling then, it was natural to look for some perennial religious value, which, like Mary's contemplation could not be taken away. The Anglican William Ralph Inge, writing one of his *Outspoken Essays* in 1914, well describes what mysticism had to offer the perplexed Christian apologist of his day:

> [The] revived belief in the inspiration of the individual has immensely strengthened the position of Christian apologists who find their old fortifications no longer tenable against the assaults of natural science and historical criticism. . . . [It] has vindicated for the spiritual life the right to stand on its own feet and rest on its own evidence. Spiritual things, we now realise, are spiritually discerned. . . . This conception of religion has much appeal today. [It brings a] relief to many who have been distressed by being told that religion is bound up with certain events in antiquity, the historicity of which is in some cases difficult to establish; with a cosmology which has been definitely disproved; and with a philosophy which they cannot make their own.[8]

Within the Roman Catholic discipline, "Modernist" was the name applied to those who adapted themselves (too quickly, the hierarchy thought) to the needed critique of scripture and dogma. Alfred Loisy, George Tyrell, Maude Petry, and Friedrich von Hügel were among the personalities of the modernist movement. The movement as a whole, though not every individual in it, was condemned by Pope Pius X in a decree, *Lamentabili Sane Exitu* (a syllabus of errors drawn from the works of Loisy and Tyrell), and the encyclical *Pascendi Dominici Gregis*—both issued in 1907.

Working under the Roman Catholic strictures of 1907, it was safer for a churchman to turn to the study of the spiritual life and to turn away from historical and critical studies that might place him under condemnation. In

1922, when von Hügel urged Cuthbert Butler to engage in critical work, Butler wrote in response:

> Years ago I recognized that these things—Xtian origins, New Testament, History of Dogma, etc.—have been made impossible for a priest, except on the most narrow apologetic lines. . . . When the Biblical Commission got under way, and the *Lamentabili* and *Pascendi* were issued, I deliberately turned away from all this work.[9]

The doctrinal uncertainty of the times encouraged the study of mysticism.

Philosophical Interest. Still another factor in the renewed interest in mysticism that began at the turn of the century was the involvement of philosophers, especially Platonists and Hegelians. William Ralph Inge's work aimed to show the Platonist base of Christian mysticism and to recommend Christian Platonism as the essence of mysticism. William Ernest Hocking, the American neo-Hegelian, concentrated on the dialectic of the mystic's experience—the mystic's ability to concentrate on "this world" with its busy demands and in other moments on "that world." If God is the Whole or Absolute, this kind of "alternation" must be necessary for anyone who lives in time and yet would "know" the Absolute. Henri Bergson in *Two Sources of Morality and Religion* (1935) was interested in the mystical as a way of viewing reality in one piece. He held that reality is dynamic and can only be seen to be so by means of intuition. Logic and the intellect inevitably dismember the whole. The intellect never sees the whole—only the segmented, manageable pieces. Evelyn Underhill adopted many of Bergson's views in *Mysticism* but later repudiated them.

Something about the philosopher's quest is itself mystical. No philosopher, not even the positivist, is satisfied with a literal, which is to say, unexamined view of reality. The fact that the philosopher undertakes his work at all shows the problematic or illusive character of the real. Philosophy, as Evelyn Underhill said, teaches "the length of its tether." The work of all philosophers is directed toward the essential limit of man's ability to know. For the scientist, the limit is a momentary arrest in an ongoing empirical conquest—a new occasion for problem solving. To the positivist, the limit marks the boundary of meaningful discourse; he who trespasses does so only on the wings of imagination and aesthetic appreciation. For the confident Thomist, the limit presents the opportunity to speak analogically. In the Kantian, the limit awakens a tempting yet irresistible fascination with what lies beyond. But to the heart of the mystic, the limit is a moment of encounter, introducing—all at once—that which is divine. There is an ultimate optimism on the part of the mystic that encourages the philosopher's quest. "Mysticism," in the words of William Ernest Hocking, "is evidently the product of an intensely philosophical spirit discontented with the mere rationality of philosophy, and of an intensely religious spirit discontented with the dogmatic systems of theology in every creed. It is inspired by the insatiable ambition of individual spirits to know reality by direct acquaintance, rather than by rumor or description."[10]

We can make two generalizations about the new critical approach to mysticism that began in the twentieth century. The first is that mysticism was studied for the sake of what it could offer men generally. What the mystics had to say must, so the assumption was, be relevant to human nature itself. Mystical experience was not studied as a rare, strange phenomenon wholly out of step with what is normal. All men, it was commonly assumed, could have "in embryo," to use a phrase of Underhill's, what the mystics had in a more intense and developed form. The second thing was the conviction that if mysticism has something to offer all men generally, then whatever is abnormal, fanatical, unhealthy, and distorted about it must be sifted out. Mysticism was not viewed simply as an unambiguously good thing. It was seen to be an enormously complex religious orientation, a bag of goods and evils. Some critical discrimination needed to be exercised first if that which was good in mysticism could be recovered. Hocking well expressed the fault that is to be found in the excesses of the *via negativa:*

> There is indeed something wrong in the theory of mysticism when it proposes the end of the Negative Path as an entire and self-sufficient good, the absolute Good. It is unjust to its own function in the world. The mystic vision, taken by itself, tends to vanish into the meaningless. Pure unity, unless it were understood to be the unity of something plural, would be a nondescript unity indistinguishable from nothing. The experience of the mystic, and the discipline that leads up to it, belong somehow in the circuits of life within the world of nature and human history[11]

This same sympathetic, critical perspective characterizes the modern interpretation of mysticism that began in 1902 with William James's *Varieties of Religious Experience.*

William James (1842–1910)

William James, along with C. S. Peirce, was the originator of American pragmatism. James's *Varieties of Religious Experience* comprises his Gifford Lectures. Partly the lectures represent the efforts of a son to come to terms with the religion of his father. Just below the surface of the assembled empirical data, one finds a man struggling with the meaning of religion in his own life. William James himself had experienced the feeling of "morbid-mindedness" that he describes in *Varieties.*

> Suddenly there fell upon me without any warning, just as if it came out of the darkness, a horrible fear of my own existence. . . . It was like a revelation, and although the immediate feelings passed away, the experience has made me sympathetic to the morbid feelings of others ever since.[12]

James's father, Henry James, Sr., was a lifelong student of theology and a disciple of Emanuel Swedenborg. Too independent to follow a conventional seminary course, he spent his life in private study. Having lost his leg in a childhood accident, James's father was never employed in a profession that made routine demands upon his time. His children grew up stimulated by family discussion, were educated here and there in private schools and under tutors, and often traveled with their parents to Europe, where they lived for short periods. At one time, William and his brother Henry studied painting seriously, and William entertained the idea of a career as an artist. Finally he settled on the study of science and medicine at Harvard, where eventually he taught physiology and anatomy, psychology and philosophy. Gertrude Stein was one of his medical students.

William James is as famous for his character as for his philosophy. His sister Alice said of him that "he would lend life and charm to a tread mill."[13] He was a master of vivid expression:

> Philosophy lives in words, but truth and fact well up into our lives in ways that exceed verbal formulation. There is in the living act of perception always something that glimmers and twinkles and will not be caught, and for which reflection comes too late. No one knows this as well as the philosopher. He must fire his volley of new vocables out of his conceptual shotgun, for his profession condemns him to this industry, but he secretly knows the hollowness and irrelevancy. His formulas are like stereoscopic or kinetoscopic photographs seen outside the instrument; they lack the depth, the motion, the vitality. In the religious sphere, in particular, belief that formulas are true can never wholly take the place of personal experience.[14]

It has been said of William and Henry James that the philospher wrote philosophy as if it were literature, and the novelist wrote literature as if it were philosophy.

The subject for William James in *The Varieties of*

Religious Experience was experience, not doctrine. James assumed a radical disjunction between religious institutions as the depository of doctrine and the individual's personal experience. Since he rejected doctrine, he assumed that to be empirical, he must focus on the individual's *private* religious feelings. It never occurred to him to study group religious experience with the tools of the sociologist. His individualism is especially evident in one of his frequently quoted definitions of religion: "The feelings, acts and experiences of individual men in their solitude, so far as they apprehend themselves to stand in relation to whatever they consider the divine." [15]

James took the stance of a physician (which he happened to be) who reports on the symptoms informally described by a great many individual patients in their own words. Just as the physician takes a medical history, James took a religious history of various individuals: George Fox, Emerson, Tolstoy, Walt Whitman—and a great many others whose names are less well known. If one is looking for strictly controlled empirical procedures, James's study of religious attitudes and feelings can hardly be called scientific.

His method of evaluating religious experience called on his philosophical pragmatism. We are to look for the validity of a religious idea by noticing what changes take place in the character of the person who entertains it. The validity, as he put it, lies in its "fruits," not in its "roots" or cause. This meant that a religious idea could not be discredited by suggesting that it originated in some physical or psychological instability. To do so was to commit a fallacy of origin that James jeeringly called "medical materialism."

In the welter of material he reports, he discerns two religious temperaments: the attitude of healthy-mindedness of the so-called once born and the morbid-mindedness of the twice born. The once born enjoy a happy uncomplicated religious temper. They sense no desperate need for salvation or deliverance. All is well and needs only to continue. Theirs is a "natural" religion of continuity, as opposed to a religion of deliverance. To the twice born, something is or has been, in their experience, radically wrong. Evil is a reality and there can be an almost desperate need to be delivered from it. Tolstoy's condition is an example of such a state. "I felt," said Tolstoy, "that something had broken within me on which my life had always rested, that I had nothing left to hold on to, and that morally my life had stopped."[16] James understood, from the inside, the condition of the morbid mind and said that religions of healthy mindedness "work" only so long as melancholy stays away.

"Conversion" is the religious name for the sick soul's recovery, and for James the significant thing about it was not its duration or suddenness, not whether it is of natural or supernatural origin, but its *effect* on the life of the person. The "fruits," or effects, of conversion he calls "sanctification" and "saintliness." "Saintliness" is "the collective name for the ripe fruits of religion in a character."[17] James describes these fruits as (1) a feeling of living in a wider world than one's own selfish interests, (2) a sense of "friendly continuity" and therefore willing self-surrender to an ideal power, (3) elation, freedom, and (4) a shift of the emotional center toward loving and harmonious affections. These are the empirical fruits of religion.

When James pauses in his reporting and evaluating to ask whether religion is "true," he is led to a more direct consideration of mysticism, or rather of mystical states. He sees mysticism not so much as a world view, as a particular "state of consciousness." This is characterized by four "marks," for which James is famous. They are (1) ineffability, (2) noetic quality, (3) transiency, and (4) passivity. He closely associates the religious and the mystical: "Personal religious experience has its root and center in mystical states of consciousness."[18] The mystical, in short, is not one type of religion or a type of philosophy but the source and ground of religious experience itself. The authority of mystical experience

James makes quite limited. It is authoritative for the person who has it but not for another. The most important thing about mystical states for James is that their existence "overthrows the pretensions" of rational, nonmystical states "to be the sole and ultimate dictators of what we may believe." They show, according to James, that rationalism is but one kind of consciousness, and they allow for the possibility of *other* orders of truth, which we may choose to believe in if something in us vitally responds to them. "It must always remain an open question whether mystical states may not possibly be such superior points of view, windows through which the mind looks out upon a more extensive and inclusive world."[19]

In looking to the effect rather than to the origin for the validation of an idea, James was free to name *mystical* any state that achieved the marks of mysticism regardless of its cause. "The drunken consciousness is one bit of the mystical consciousness," he said. "Nitrous oxide and ether, especially nitrous oxide, when diluted with air, stimulate the mystical consciousness in an extraordinary degree."[20] Drug-induced states were not a central feature of James's study of mysticism, but the fact that he had a philosophy that did not preclude their consideration has made him something of a pioneer for today's drug cultists. To Evelyn Underhill, Baron von Hügel, and Dean Inge, all of whom worked from a more idealist, less pragmatic philosophical base, James's point of view was distorted.

It is important to realize that James is led to a serious consideration of mysticism, or rather of mystical "states," because he undertakes to describe the individual religious *experience*. He takes little notice of mysticism as a type of philosophy or a metaphysical world view. He is interested in the mystical as an indication that there is something *more* implied or felt whenever an individual has a religious experience. His pragmatism disposes him to look for whatever can be put into effective use by the individual who, like James himself, is tossed about by life's highs and lows. What helpful frame of mind can one consciously adopt without sacrificing one's intellectual integrity? This was the question that expressed his own struggle. He never directly asks if what the mystic experiences is an objective reality. His method requires him to leave that question unanswered. His is a managerial conception that derives from his pragmatism. With what idea can we go forward to meet what life deals out, and what is the intellectual justification for entertaining such an idea? The mystic state gives him a clue to the answer. It is possible, but by no means proven, that there is a something more, a wider world to which man is given access in that ground of religious experience called the mystical state. In the absence of proofs to the contrary, we are justified, on pragmatic grounds, in directing our lives in accordance with this more.

The fact that James keeps to religious experience as his theme is an advantage in one important respect. He need not determine the objectivity of the matters under discussion. His purely descriptive method is confined to putting on display the religious experience men say they have and the difference they say it makes to them. The bracing honesty of his intention is inspiring and worthy of the emulation of all who undertake philosophical inquiry into religious themes. His pragmatic and managerial outlook, however, discourages the consideration of mysticism as a philosophy in its own right, not of management but of vision. James's interest in mysticism is at odds with the enterprise of the mystics themselves. His interest was not in what we must inescapably believe to be true but in what we may legitimately entertain as possibly true.

Chapter 6
Classic Modern Interpreters

In 1927, when Rudolf Otto lectured on mysticism at King's College, London, he told his audience that to lecture on mysticism in England was to bring "owls to Athens" or "coals to Newcastle." Otto attributed the mystical nature of religion in England to the influence of the Book of Common Prayer, and he indicated his interest in producing a similar book for the German people.[1] It is hard to say whether Otto was right about English religious life or simply patronizing his audience. But the three writers we now consider would lend support to his statement. All were English. They are Evelyn Underhill, William Ralph Inge, and Friedrich von Hügel. Two were Anglicans, and one was Roman Catholic.

Evelyn Underhill was a minor poet, novelist, and journalist, who also taught a university course in mysticism. She was the only child of an aristocratic family and was educated in private schools and at King's College, London. She was married to Stuart Moore, an admiralty lawyer. Her religious upbringing was Anglican and seemingly only formal until, on a retreat at St. Mary of the Angels in Southampton, she underwent a conversion experience. She then became strongly attracted to Roman Catholicism and sought the advice of von Hügel about converting. He advised her against a hasty decision, and eventually she chose not to make the change. One factor in her decision was the suppression of Catholic Modernism in 1907, what seemed to her to be a curtailment of intellectual honesty in Roman Catholicism.

Evelyn Underhill brought to the study of mysticism a clarity of journalistic style and a depth of learning. Her interpretive classic, *Mysticism* (1911), helped remove the subject from the shelf of esoterica and make it available to the general reader. Her theological direction in that book is strongly theocentric, as distinguished from Christocentric. She had some intellectual scruples that led her to ask: How can an object of worship be at the same time an item of historical research and therefore uncertain? In the 1920s she carried on a correspondence with von Hügel in which these difficulties were aired. To von Hügel (and later to herself) her book *Mysticism* seemed too negligent of externals and of the outer "husk" and form—the institutional factor in religion. Externals, von Hügel told her, seemed to her to be "mere" externals. One of her later works, *The Life of the Spirit* (1922), is more appreciative of the institutional factor.

Far less wary of neglecting externals was William Ralph Inge. Of the three writers we consider, Inge is the only clergyman, and in many ways, he is the most critical of churchly officialdom and external form. He was the Anglican dean of St. Paul's Cathedral. His major scholarly works include *The Philosophy of Plotinus* (1918), *Christian Mysticism* (1899), *Personal Idealism and Mysticism* (1907), *Studies of English Mystics* (1906), and *Mysticism in Religion* (1948). He was a gifted essayist and polemicist, who earned the name "the gloomy Dean." The following passages from his *Outspoken Essays,* written around World War I, testify to the appropriateness of his nickname:

> The Churches, and especially the Church of England, have gone from bad to worse. The number of clergy, which

was once about 24,000 has sunk to 18,500, although all
other professions are crowded, and the bishops reject very
few applications. . . .

[Organized religion] has been a failure ever since the
first concordat between Church and State under Constan-
tine the Great. [We must] distinguish sharply between
ecclesiasticism, theology, and religion.[2]

As to the overscrupulosity of refusing "an inward call to
the ministry" because it requires formal assent "to
unsuitably worded texts drawn up three centuries ago,"
Inge says, "An obstinate persistence in that kind of
honesty would have excluded from the ministry all
except fools, liars, and bigots." Bishop Gore "makes a
fetish of the creeds, documents which only represent the
opinions of a majority at a meeting." Christianity, Inge
held, "is a form of idealism; and idealism means belief in
absolute or spiritual values."[3] Inge did not hesitate to opt
for spirit *at the expense* of externals.

Inge's brand of Christian idealism put him at some
distance from the position of Friedrich von Hügel, who
especially emphasized the religious value of externals—
"the thing-element," in religion. Von Hügel thought a
major aberration in mysticism was its neglect of needed
externals. Spirit and "thing" should not exclude each
other. Von Hügel was an English Catholic lay theologian.
His major work, *The Mystical Element of Religion*
(1908), a study of St. Catherine of Genoa, had as its chief
theme the relationship of the personal and the mystical.
Von Hügel was a liberal Catholic of his time and, in
accord with the Catholic Modernists, thought the
hierarchy of his day failed to appreciate the work of
biblical scholarship and, in its doctrinal formulations,
compromised its results. His mother was English, but his
father had been an Austrian diplomat, and he inherited
the honorary title "Baron." Von Hügel had an interna-
tional acquaintance and correspondence with leading
religious thinkers, both Catholic and Protestant. As we
have indicated, he was a special friend and adviser of

Evelyn Underhill, who asked him to act in the capacity of her spiritual director. In his reinterpretation of the mystical tradition of Christianity, he stressed the need to understand the mystics' *One* more in terms of an integrated personality than a Neoplatonist and Pseudo-Dionysian abstraction.

These three thinkers were acquainted with one another and had something to say of one another's work. Dean Inge thought that Underhill was disproportionate in her interest in practical mysticism, to the neglect of mysticism as a philosophy of Platonist idealism. Inge's own interest in Christian apologetics led him to praise von Hügel's *Mystical Element* as a great work in this area. Puzzled, von Hügel replied that he felt like a dog who had won a prize in a cat show. Von Hügel's interest in mysticism did not stem from apologetics. In fact, he spurned any crudely practical purpose in his scholarship. "After all, there exist poets' poets, do there not? Why not then also writers' writers or thinkers' thinkers?"[4] Von Hügel never wrote for popular consumption, and except for his letters, he requires a tenacious reader. He was capable here and there of an extraordinarily illuminating phrase, but his Germanic style was hampered by overly careful qualification of every statement. The result was pronounced "barbaric" by Dean Inge, who was a craftsman of the elegant English sentence. All three were appreciative and yet critical of William James's effort in *Varieties of Religious Experience*. Underhill bridled at James's inclusion of drugs and intoxication. Inge and von Hügel both thought that James's approach by way of psychology tended to exaggerate the abnormal and odd experience in mysticism.[5] Each of the interpreters we are considering wished to reclaim mysticism for the common man. The mystic's apprehension was not, they thought, ultimately irrational, but a deepening of reason itself. If one phrase will serve to name the interpretive premise of each, it is the *continuity of reason* in mysticism.

Evelyn Underhill (1875–1941)

William James's interest in mysticism had largely centered on an empirical description of the individual mystic's *state* of consciousness and not on the history of mystical literature. He drew his materials seemingly at random from any individual who reported having had a religious experience. Evelyn Underhill deals with her subject the way a literary critic deals with his. She cares deeply about it, and at the same time her critical faculties are enormously sensitive. She was an Anglican churchman, but she did not write in the manner of a theologian subject to the constraints of church doctrine. Although most of her examples are drawn from Christian sources, she defined mysticism broadly as an "intensive form" of the "essential religious experience of man." Mysticism is "the expression of the innate tendency of the human spirit towards complete harmony with the transcendental order; by whatever the theological formula under which that order is understood." It makes no difference whether the end of the mystic's quest is called God, World Soul, or Absolute, it is mystical so long as the movement toward it "is a genuine process and not an intellectual speculation."[6]

We can expect from Underhill, then, the commentary of one who is greatly sensitive to religious experience herself, one who defines "mystical" as an intense form of the religious experience that is open to all men. She characterizes the mystical as practical and not speculative, by which she means (although she did not have the usage available) existentially involved, not detached. "In mysticism that love of truth which we saw as the beginning of all philosophy leaves the merely intellectual sphere, and takes on the assured aspect of a personal passion. . . . Hence whilst the Absolute of the metaphysician remains a diagram—impersonal and unattainable—the Absolute of the mystics is lovable, attainable, alive." "Not to *know about,* but to *Be,* is the mark of the real initiate."[7]

In answer to William James's four marks of mysticism, Evelyn Underhill provides four rules, or "notes," which she intends to serve as a definition of mysticism.[8] We can, here and there, indicate points of departure from James, but Underhill's notes do not appear to be an exact contrast to James's four marks.

1. "Mysticism is practical, not theoretical." Mysticism is "a something which the whole self does; not something as to which the intellect holds an opinion." "Over and over again the great mystics tell us, not how they speculated, but how they acted." Mysticism is not a philosophy although it can provide the substance "upon which mystical philosophy cogitates."[9]

Here her primary concern is to say that mysticism is active and not passive. By "active," however, she means that mysticism is something the whole person *does;* it is not just a theory he passively entertains. James, of course, had made passivity a mark of the mystical state, but it is well to remember that he had in mind the mystic's state of consciousness and not the whole mystical enterprise and effort. The question should be raised as to whether what is "theoretical" and "intellectual" is fairly represented by Underhill as "passive." Is a theory "entertained" only by a part of the self (an intellectual faculty)? Is there no engagement of the whole person? We shall later find Dean Inge with a different view.

2. "Mysticism is an entirely Spiritual Activity." We are not to look to the empirical world for the confirmation or "use" of mysticism. The mystic's purpose is not "to improve and elucidate the visible by help of the invisible"; it is not "to use the supernormal powers of the self for the increase of power, virtue, happiness or knowledge."[10]

Underhill does not say so, but this note is applicable to James's having found the "fruits" of religious experience to be its validating test. To look for this kind of use and empirical validation is, in Underhill's opinion, to move toward "magic and magical religion," even though religious experience may (like James's "Mind-Cure"?) be magic in its "exalted and least materialistic form." [11]

The distinction between mysticism and magic was a special point with Underhill, particularly because mysticism was and always has been popularly associated with magic. Magic, she held, has in view the *use* to which it can put its gained transcendental knowledge. It looks above in order to turn its gaze to some self-advantage. The mystic, in contrast, "possesses God, and needs nothing more." "Magic wants to get, mysticism wants to give." In magic the "will unites with the intellect in an impassioned desire for supersensible knowledge. This is the intellectual, aggressive, and scientific temperament trying to extend its field of consciousness, until it includes the supersensual world: obviously the antithesis of mysticism, though often adopting its title and style." [12] The hallmark of mysticism as opposed to magic is that mysticism is generous and not self-serving. The next note, or rule, of mysticism identifies this generous feature of mysticism as love.

3. "The business and method of Mysticism is Love." The mystic is moved toward a "personal Object of Love" which is "never an object of exploration." [13] By "Love," Underhill tells us she means, not a sentiment, but a "total dedication of the will," a "life movement of the self." "It is the eager, outgoing activity whose driving power is generous love, not the absorbent, indrawing activity which strives only for new knowledge." [14] Love, then, is a movement that involves the *whole self,* and it effects changes in a person's character as a whole. It is this total effect and the pilgrimage of the whole person (the Mystic Way) that she has in mind in the next, the fourth note of mysticism—however vague the sentence may read when it stands alone and unexplained:

4. "Mysticism entails a definite Psychological Experience." "Living union" with the One which is sought in love is an enhancement of the whole of one's life. It is "arrived at by an arduous psychological and spiritual process—the so-called 'Mystic Way'—entailing the com-

plete remaking of character and the liberation of a new, or rather latent form of consciousness." It is sometimes inaccurately called "ecstasy," or better, the "Unitive State." Mysticism involves the reorganizing and rebuilding of the whole self, not just an emotional or intellectual apprehension.[15]

The second half of Evelyn Underhill's *Mysticism* is devoted to a description of the educative process indicated in this fourth note—the Mystic Way.[16] *Conversion* is the name of the initial stage of the process. It is an "awakening" of the self to a consciousness of Divine Reality. It is marked by joy and a shift of gaze from the lower to higher. It may be gradual, but it is often accompanied by some "travail." In the second stage of *Purgation,* or *Purification,* the self realizes its unfitness in contrast to the reality it beholds. It therefore seeks to remove its unfitness by adopting, as is often the case, some form of ascetic practice of "Mortification" of some ordinary desires. *Illumination* is the beginning of the contemplative state, a state of happiness but not yet full Union. It is to be compared, Underhill says, to Plato's cave dwellers' first emergence from the cave; it is a looking at the sun. It gives promise of a fuller realization to come. The final stage, *Unitive Life,* is "the life in which man's will is united with God."[17] The metaphysical mystic describes it as deification in impersonal terms. The intimate mystic describes it in terms of spiritual marriage. Both convey something essentially the same. The only difference is one of temperament.

Just as there is a progression in the mystic's education from an awakening to a full unitive life, there is a progression in his meditations and prayers. Underhill warns us, however, that the "degrees" of prayer are often cataloged too neatly by the mystics and that their divisions are "largely artificial and symbolic." St. Teresa's classifications of prayer are "far from lucid" and vary with their representations in different works. In describing the stages of prayer, one should stress prayer as a "coherent process" that amounts to the education of the self.[18]

The "introversion" of prayer can be studied under three heads: recollection, quiet, and contemplation. In simple form these stages can be experienced by anyone "in embryo" if he will (1) make an act of concentration (recollection), (2) sense silence (quiet), and (3) attain thereby a new perception (contemplation). Roughly the correlation between the manner of prayer and stage of the mystic's life is:

Meditation—Purification stage
Quiet—Illuminative stage
Contemplation proper—Close upon the attainment
                of the Unitive State.[19]

As we see, then, Evelyn Underhill represents mysticism as a practice, as a process the whole self undergoes. Mysticism as a philosophy is a secondary reflection upon this prior raw material. Mystical philosophy is "the comment of the intellect on the proceedings of spiritual intuition."[20] When she does move to discuss secondary reflections on the mystic's experience, she sets up two types of theory, *emanation* and *immanence*.

Emanation postulates a separation between God and man and implies the inaccessibility of God. It maximizes the transcendence of God. It accords with James's "sick soul," which seeks some remedy to its radical estrangement. The quest for God is long and hard.

Immanence is the type of theory that holds that the quest of the Absolute is not a long journey but a realization of something implicit. It comports with James's "healthy-minded" religion. It celebrates the presence of God, not his inaccessibility. Taken alone, immanence can degenerate into pantheism and into the simple identification (deification) of soul and God.

When mysticism is understood as a spiritual quest, there are three symbols by which the quest can be understood or illuminated. And, in many ways, Underhill's chapter "Mysticism and Symbolism," in which she discusses these three ways, is one of the most illuminating in the book.

The first set of symbols envisions the mystic's progress in terms of a long, hard journey toward a known and definite goal—the idea of a pilgrimage of which Dante's *Divine Comedy* and Bunyan's *Pilgrim's Progress* would be examples. Man is depicted with a restless longing to go out from his normal world in search of a lost home. This set of symbols parallels the doctrine of emanation.

The second set of symbols makes the relationship intimate and personal and employs the imagery of love and marriage. Here, the intimacy desired is most naturally compared to human love.

The third set of symbols elaborates the doctrine of immanence. These are symbols that depict an introspective look into the self and the discernment of a kinship between the self and that which is its end. The self desires intimacy with that which is perfect and aims, therefore, at making itself perfect. It is ascetic. Man's moral character is likened to the alchemist's metal. Just as a "latent goldness" lies buried in the metal, so a spiritual goldness lies hidden in the man.

Purely speculative mysticism suffers some denigration at the hands of Underhill because she fails to appreciate the experiential and practical basis of the impulse to press on to ultimate conclusions and ends. Speculation seems detached and devoid of experiential content. An early dependence on Bergson's vitalism (later repudiated) underscores this characterization of speculation. The doctrine of the mystics "must be founded in the first instance on what they know by experience of the relation between that Absolute and the individual self." "Since Mysticism is a way of life—an experience of Reality, not a philosophic account of Reality—Neoplatonism, and the mysticism which used its language, must not be identified with one another."[21]

To Evelyn Underhill the value of mysticism lay in what it disclosed of humanity in general. "Every person, then, who awakens to consciousness of a Reality which transcends the normal world of sense—however small, weak, imperfect that consciousness may be—is put upon a road which follows at low levels the path which the mystic treads at high levels."[22]

William Ralph Inge (1860–1954)

The Anglican William Ralph Inge was through and through a Christian Platonist. In his major work, *Christian Mysticism,* he adopts a historical method and puts before the reader critical discussions of the great Christian mystics and their schools. Inge held that "the blend of Neoplatonism and New Testament Christianity" provides the best basis for a Christian apologetic in his day.[23] He was steeped in the philosophy of Plotinus, and when he used words like "reason" and "rational," they always had reference to their usage in Plotinus. His interest in mysticism was that of a philosophical idealist who wishes to discern the "Truth" and who saw the closest kinship between the philosopher's enterprise and that of the mystics.

What is it that Platonism furnishes the interpreter of mysticism? What is the philosophical basis of the mystic's aim? It lies along two lines. The philosophical idealist and the mystic both assume a separation between what is present and what is beyond. There is, then, a *distinction*. The second thing consistently stressed by Inge is that while there is a distinction, there is also a *continuity* between "this world" and "that world." Platonism and mysticism both see man as stretched between the two worlds, and both find, above all, that there is some continuity between the two worlds. Inge absolutely rejects any notion of Platonism as an intractable dualism. He finds the contribution of Platonism to be the distinction *and* continuity between the two worlds.

We find Inge, again and again, concluding that that mysticism is best which most clearly sees the continuity between the two worlds. He has no sympathy with mysticism defined as a miraculous intervention from a supernatural realm or as essentially irrational. Mysticism is a quest of the human spirit that is entirely normal and in the broadest, Neoplatonist sense *rational*. His clearest characterization of mysticism stresses these two points—the distinction and the continuity of the two worlds.

> Mysticism has its origin in that which is the raw material of all religion, and perhaps of all philosophy and art as well, namely, that dim consciousness of the *beyond*, which is part of our nature as human beings. . . . Mysticism may be defined as the attempt to realise the presence of the living God in the soul and in nature, or, more generally, *as the attempt to realise in thought and feeling, the immanence of the temporal in the eternal, and of the eternal in the temporal.*[24]

Since a critical perspective characterizes the studies we are considering, we can find it easier to get to the given view of mysticism by asking what the writer thinks is wrong with mysticism. What is there in it that needs correcting, and along what lines does the correction lie? That which Inge thought needed to be corrected was too sharp an opposition between the natural and the supernatural. He believed that overdrawing the line of demarcation had several undesirable results.

One is that it leads toward the excesses of the *via negativa*, whereby God is pushed above being altogether. God is stripped of all attributes until nothing remains but a point; the point too is removed because it is a numerical unit, and God is above this.[25]

Another result is an inordinate concern with asceticism and the suppression of the body. "While an almost morbid desire to suffer is found in many [mystics], there is nothing in the system itself to encourage men to maltreat their bodies." Asceticism, Inge thinks, is an accidental attachment to mysticism, not an essential feature of it. Asceticism is too individualizing. When it is regarded as a virtue or duty in itself, it tends, he says, to isolate us and concentrate attention on the separate self.

"This is contrary to the spirit of Mysticism, which aims at realising unity and solidarity everywhere." The "monkish asceticism" of the Middle Ages depends on a dualistic view "which does not belong to the essence of Mysticism."[26]

Another concomitant of the overdrawn dualism between nature and supernature is the use of the so-called miraculous as a kind of material evidence for the supernatural. If nature and spirit were seen to be distinguished yet interwoven, then spirit would be implied in everything natural. If they are severed from each other, then spirit can find access to the natural only by a totally unnatural interruption, a miracle. Inge steadily argues against making miracle a matter of evidence for belief, a habit of mind that, in a polemical spirit, he identifies with the typical Roman Catholic view of his day. Mysticism, in Inge's understanding of it, has nothing to do with the unnatural intrusions of a spiritual world into a natural world that is alien to it. It has to do with the natural and rational inference to spirit that arises from the natural world. The historicity of the miracles in the Gospels and creeds, he says, is a scientific and not a religious question. "To make our belief in Christ as a living and life-giving Spirit depend on any abnormal occurrences in the physical world seems to me to be an undetected residue of materialism." The sharp distinction between nature and supernature sets up a "craving" for physical "mystical phenomena to support the belief in supernatural interventions."[27] Such an irrationalism abandons the doctrine of Logos as a cosmic principle.

> It ushers us into an entirely new world, where the familiar criteria of truth and falsehood are inapplicable. And what it reveals to us is not a truer and deeper view of the actual, but a wholly independent cosmic principle which invades the world of experience as a disturbing force, spasmodically subverting the laws of nature in order to show its power over them.[28]

The Spanish mystics St. Teresa and St. John of the Cross, in Inge's view, entirely sacrificed the needed continuity in favor of such an irrationality. "The inner light which they sought was not an illumination of the intellect in its search for truth, but a consuming fire to burn up all earthly passions and desires. . . . They were ascetics first and Church Reformers next; neither of them was a typical mystic." [29] It is surprising to find the Spanish mystics so summarily dismissed. Timid qualifications were never a part of Inge's style! For Inge it is the presence of Platonism that makes a mystic "typical"; its supposed absence in St. Teresa and St. John of the Cross makes him wave them off as "irrational," atypical mystics.

If the best sort of mysticism is a Platonism, then for Inge there can be no essential conflict between mysticism and reason understood in the Platonist sense. Mysticism, at its best, is a kind of Platonism the basis of which is "reason above rationalism, reason (*nous* or *intellectus*) being used for the affirmations of the whole personality acting under the guidance of its highest faculty." By *reason* Inge would have us understand "something much higher than logic-chopping; it can provide, from its own resources, a remedy for the intellectual error that is just now miscalled intellectualism." "Reason is, or should be, the logic of our entire personality, and . . . if Reason is so defined, it does not come into conflict with Mysticism." [30]

A number of alleged theological pitfalls in mysticism cause Inge little concern and represent to him cries of wolf where there is no wolf. Inge is quick to dismiss any threat from mysticism to the church's institutional life. Whatever is reforming and, therefore, disruptive about mysticism should be risked in order to appropriate mysticism's needed reforming spirit. Mysticism is a reformation—a "revival of spirituality in the midst of formalism or unbelief." [31] Even as a churchman, Inge was delightfully bombastic in his criticisms of institutional religion. About 1914, he wrote:

Organized Christianity is at present under a cloud. The Churches have but little influence, and if they had more they would not know what to do with it.

I believe . . . that the aberrations or exaggerations of institutionalism have been and are, more dangerous, and further removed from the spirit of Christianity than those of mysticism, and that we must look to the latter type, rather than to the former, to give life to the next religious revival.[32]

Pantheism is another danger that Inge thinks is exaggerated. Pantheism is "a pitfall for mysticism to avoid, not an error involved in its first principles." In any event, it is better to take the benefits that mysticism offers even if there is an accompanying risk of pantheism. More risk attends an overdrawn nature-spirit dualism. Inge concludes that if pantheism simply means an outright identification of God with the totality of existence, then such a conception is found only in Indian religion and not at all in Christian Platonism. If pantheism means the identification of God with a dynamic cosmic process, then pantheism is not mystical either: mystics like Eckhart, who spoke of God in terms of a process never, he says, made it a "temporal process."[33]

A third false danger in mysticism is the special topic of Inge's *Idealism and Mysticism* (1907), which comprised the Paddock Lectures he delivered in the United States. In it he takes issue with the overly strict individualism of early pragmatism and personal idealism. Does mysticism entail the absorption of the individual into a larger whole and the loss of personal moral responsibility? Inge thinks that the danger of such a thing is exaggerated. He is especially critical of those who, in reaction to such a danger, think of personality as an "impervious" pellet of matter. As in all things, he looks to Plotinus to tell him what personality is. It is not that which man is given to start with and which he must defend against the claims of others. It is something he develops as he grows. The

Neoplatonist view of personality, and that of their Christian disciples, is that "unification of the personality is a gradual process, coincident with our growth in grace." Personality is an ideal, not a given fact. We acquire personality with patience. "And the paradox lies in this, that the way to gain it is to lose it." Atomistic imperviousness of personality is asserted out of a concern for moral responsibility. But spiritual things are not outside or inside each other. Christian faith does "not believe on a Person; it believes in and through him: it becomes . . . participant with him and through him of a force of life and conduct." Inge says the God-man relationship that is spoken of in the New Testament as "indwelling," "membership," and "union" is as adequately described as can be done with words.[34]

Inge is more afraid of a hard individuality than of losing the self in absorption. It is possible, he thinks, to save personality "without regarding the human spirit as a monad, independent and sharply separated from other spirits. Distinction, not separation, is the mark of personality." To be sure, the mystics are wrong to have simply substituted the Divine for human nature. The self of our immediate consciousness is *not* our true personality. We *attain* personality as "spiritual and rational beings" by "passing beyond the limits which mark us off as separate individuals. Separate individuality, we may say, is the bar which prevents us from realising our true privilege as persons."[35] Losing the individuality, the monadic conception of the self, is prerequisite to finding true life, which is an expansion of the personal.

Friedrich von Hügel (1852–1925)

Von Hügel is a critic of mysticism, but an enamored critic. He supposed that mysticism is a general need or an answer to a generally felt need. It is a way of being religious that pervades human nature overall. But it must be qualified and corrected in some way. It must be cured of its nihilism, of its "unhealthy" elements, of its ethical indifference, of its social isolationism. Mysticism, then, is

a doctrine and a phenomenon with a mixture of
strengths and weaknesses. In von Hügel's diagnosis of
what is wrong with mysticism, he focuses on its overly
geometric view of unity. Too often, as we have seen with
Eckhart, the Plotinian One, as the end of the mystics'
contemplative quest, became a simple blank circle out of
reach of all distinctions. When the view of unity is too
simple man's spirituality can be kept "pure" only by
placing his this-worldly interests outside the circumference of the circle. When the mystic conceives the idea of
his end too geometrically, he is drawn into an uncompromising otherworldliness and, at times, into ethical
irresponsibility. Von Hügel works to reinterpret the idea
of unity as a "unity-in-diversity." He proposes the
"personal," or "personality," as the prototype of a better, a
more dynamic, nongeometrical kind of unity.

In his work of reinterpretation, von Hügel describes
three elements of religious life that, he says, must be
brought into unity without negating the special contribution of each.[36]

The first, the *institutional* element, he describes
variously as the external, authoritative, factual, historical, and institutional side of religion. This side accepts
facts unreflectively and innocently, like a child. The
second, the rational, reflective, *philosophical* side, is to be
compared to the questioning of the youth; the innocent
acceptance of facts is replaced by a thoughtful scrutiny
of them. The third, the *emotive-intuitive* element, is
likened to the emotional-volitional-experimental side of
the mature man. Here religion is "loved and lived rather
than analyzed." These three elements, or "forces," he
also compares to three emphases in the church's
institutional life: the parties—High Church, Broad
Church and Evangelical—are roughly representative, in
their respective emphases, of the institutional, the
philosophical, and the emotive elements. Among Roman
Catholic orders the identifications are Jesuits, authoritative; Dominicans, speculative; and Franciscans, emotive.

While von Hügel speaks of these as disparate elements, he also asserts that each is always accompanied by some amount of the other two. Religion is always a combination of these, and it is the *person* who combines them into a living whole. But they are living forces, and their harmonization is never fully finished in the way that a "dead mosaic" of static elements could be finished.

The mystical element of religion is not to be understood as simply one of these three elements but rather as an overall urge to unify diverse influences such as these. An aberrant tendency of mysticism is that it seeks to unify the elements too simply. By settling on one and disregarding others, the mystic wrongly tries to escape what von Hügel thought of as a healthful "friction." The mystic may fix on some institutional practice such as the sacrament, or on some philosophical idea like Being. He may, especially in mystical lyricism, focus on the emotional satisfactions of the contemplative life. If, however, the mystic tries to achieve his unity by avoiding all mixture of these three elements, he does not achieve the *unity-in-diversity* von Hügel has in mind. He becomes narrow and fanatical and suffers a "stunting" of his personality.

The practical application of these ideas in von Hügel's spiritual counsel and letters was that he often advised his correspondents to pursue some purely *secular* interest. This was a special emphasis of his advice to Evelyn Underhill. He thought that the secular had an importance for the religious. One is not more religious simply by attending more and more to religion as a special subject or activity. Von Hügel, in fact, had worked out rather thoroughly the theme that Dietrich Bonhoeffer had time to treat only fragmentarily—the religious value of the secular.

The theme of much of von Hügel's writing, and especially of *The Mystical Element of Religion,* is that the person or personality is a better analogue of unity than the mystics' geometric analogue, the circle or the One. Personality is precisely a living rather than geometric unity, and it can sustain conflicting elements with some cost, pain, or tension, but never, except in the fanatic, with so much tension that the unity is destroyed. It is in sustaining this living unity and bearing the tensions this necessitates that the incipient person grows to be even more of a "person" and grows toward an approximation of the perfect personality exemplified only in God. The view is like Inge's, except that where von Hügel emphasizes the importance of externals and "things" for the growth of the person, Inge would renounce them in the interest of spirit. Von Hügel never satisfactorily defined *person* or *the personal*. Unacquainted with modern personality theory, he naïvely assumed that any "person," as he understood the word, would know the meaning of these terms.

The relationship of nature to supernature is represented by von Hügel as a continuum, and in this he agrees with Inge and Underhill. "Nature draws us to God, as the dim, though most real background and groundwork of our existence; and Supernature raises this semi-conscious affinity to an active hunger for direct and clear vision, for a true participation in the Supernatural Life of God." Von Hügel would, accordingly, reject the idea of the total corruption of human nature, and he warns against interpreting Christianity so christocentrically as to deprive it of "dim apprehension, formless recollection, pictureless emotion, and the sense of the Hiddenness and Transcendence of the very God, Who is Immanent and Self-Revealing, in various degrees and ways, in every place and time."[37]

As a consequence of this assumed continuity, von Hügel, like Inge, rejects discontinuity—the sudden, the miraculous or abnormal—as a reliable indicator of the supernatural. The spiritual life "even in its fullest Christian development" is "essentially not miraculous but supernatural." He therefore thought it is possible to discover certain "laws" by which one can grow in the spiritual life—an assumption that lends his writing the authoritative air of one who advises others from out of his own spiritual discoveries.[38] Some of von Hügel's writing took a form that would seem patronizing today—that of spiritual advice-giving to friends and correspondents. Of this type, the best known examples are his collection *Letters of Baron von Hügel to a Niece* and his two-volume series, *Essays and Addresses.*

The reinterpretation of unity that von Hügel recommends has several implications for Christian ethics:

1. A unity-in-diversity will allow and encourage a variety of interests and ends. While there may be a tension between this-worldly and that-worldly ends, this tension need not become the destructive conflict it would necessarily become if these ends were regarded as competing for "space" within a circle. Cultural, social, and moral activities, not directly religious in nature, may be accorded a positive usefulness to the religious life itself.

2. There need be no conflict between person and thing. If person is understood as a unity-in-diversity, then that which is personal cannot be defined in such a way that it contrasts absolutely with things. Seemingly impersonal things—creeds, historical facts, institutions, as well as secular interests—are indeed found to be among the elements that constitute personal unity. Von Hügel thought that an attempt to do away with these necessary externals (the "thing-element") positively jeopardized the personal.

3. With the reinterpretation of unity, the action of man and the action of God are less likely to be regarded as two forces in competition. It becomes less important to keep a strict accounting of whether it is *I* who act or God who acts. Such a competition is not necessary, von Hügel thinks, if the action of God is conceived as "operating in and through and with our own." It is artificial and unnecessary to require choosing between man's initiative and man's receptivity.

4. We recall how, in Meister Eckhart, the ethical aim became detachment or disinterestedness (*Abgescheidenheit*)—a total lack of self-interest and a renunciation of all distinctions of value. All things are alike when

seen in the light of God—such was Eckhart's conviction. Von Hügel thought not only that this kind of ethical distinterestedness needed to be corrected but that it could be corrected with his own less geometric way of thinking. One did not need to try to preserve the sanctity of what the mystics called "Pure Love" by removing it altogether from some degree of self-interest or from the necessary exercise of discriminating judgment.

Von Hügel is a mystic-personalist. He believes that, far from swallowing the self, mysticism at its best develops the personal in religion. The best and most developed personality has an apprehension of the eternal and simultaneous *while* it is engaged in its contact with the wide variety of external "things" furnished by actual living. One does not apprehend "that world" by taking flight from "this world." Indeed, to regard total disengagement as necessary was a mistake of "false" or uncritical mysticism, whose concept of unity made it possible to see the eternal only as excluding externals. Its asceticism constituted an impoverishment of the personality, which is, in fact, enriched rather than impoverished by the stimulus of externals. Nevertheless, such contact should not be a simple busy occupation with externals but rather "action" instead of "activity." This requires an appropriate kind of asceticism—one which acknowledges that some pain and suffering is an inevitable accompaniment of growth, but which on no account would allow suffering to be an end in itself or to be regarded in any way as good. [39]

A geometrically conceived unity, having a quite fixed circumference, must always provoke either-or, all-or-nothing choices. It achieves a tidy intellectualism and clarity at the cost of preempting the untidy "richness" of actual experience. In contrast, an organically conceived unity may invite the healthy stimulus of shades of difference and conflict and thus be more faithful to what is signified both by the actual rough-and-tumble nature of human experience and the immediate, real, though dim, apprehension of the eternal in experience. It acknowledges a mystery of mist, a "confused knowledge" of "rich" reality. Love, even Pure Love need not ignore or disengage itself from other ends of self-advantage or motive—provided such ends do not become controlling. A more ample view of unity may include within it both recipiency and action. There can be a continuum between that which lies inherent in the human heart and prompts it to be receptive, and that which is disclosed to it by virtue of divine initiative. Mysticism, thus corrected, prompts the development of the *person* while at the same time encouraging his apprehension of transcendence in that divine discontent he perceives within his person.

Continuity, Discontinuity, and the Personal

In summary, it is possible to say that, whatever the differences of detail, each of the modern interpreters agrees that mysticism can go wrong, and each broadly agrees on the corrective. What can be seen as wrong with mysticism is an exaggerated discontinuity between nature and spirit, between man and God, between man's normal rational discernments and the in-breaking of spiritual illumination. All three critics reject a gross asceticism and an uncompromising negative path that falls over the brink into nihilism. Mysticism, they all agree, must somehow speak to the inhabitants of "this world," however much it speaks of a "that world" implied by this one. All three interpreters would recommend something like "continuity" as the needed corrective to "false" or distorted mysticism. Discontinuity is the name of what can go wrong with mysticism. What will put it right is continuity. Mysticism at its best has precisely this continuity to offer. The *impersonalness* of mysticism, which represents one of its unwanted aberrations, is occasioned by discontinuity. The cure lies in continuity, wherein lies also the recovery of the personal in mysticism.

We could rest secure with this conclusion as to how the mystical is related to the personal, if it were not for the fact that another set of thinkers takes precisely the opposite tack. For the I-Thou theologians, continuity is, in a word, what is wrong with mysticism and is what causes the personal to be forced out. The personal, they say, is driven out or swallowed up by the mystical. In the next chapter we need to think about this issue of such primary importance for Christian mysticism. How is the mystical related to the personal?

PART FOUR
Issues and Observations

A person can hardly know that he knows God when he does not know himself! This much is certain: when a man is happy, happy to the core of beatitude, he is no longer conscious of himself or anything else. He is conscious only of God.

—Meister Eckhart

Chapter 7
The Mystical
and the Personal

Often in history, the mystic has made trouble for the theologian. During those periods when the theologian discharged his responsibilities as an arm of the authoritative church, the mystic, guided by his inward light, seemed too easily to abandon external authority. When the theologian tried to meet his responsibility by centering attention on man's ethical life, mysticism seemed too ineffective and otherworldly. If the theologian stressed the individualism of man, mysticism seemed too easily to absorb him in an all-embracing One or Absolute. To the theologian who stressed the objectivity and transcendence of the Christian revelation, mysticism seemed too subjective. If the content of faith was presented as a relationship to one who says "thou" mysticism seemed to be an impersonal relationship with an *It,* a divine substance.

The key question for any evaluation of mysticism by Christian theology is how mysticism is related to the personal. The interpreters of mysticism we have just examined appropriate many, though not all, elements of mysticism. They do so in the confidence that mysticism, approached critically, can support and strengthen the personal. As we shall see, the I-Thou theologians reject mysticism altogether and do so because they believe

mysticism is depersonalizing. The conflicting evaluations of mysticism are, of course, determined by the way
that the personal is described in the two philosophies.
But the reactions of both groups strongly suggest that
the test, the theoretical condition of a *Christian* mysticism, is the presence in it of that element, however
defined, that signifies the personal.

The Personal Interpreted as I-Thou Encounter

Martin Buber, the great Jewish philosopher, provided
Christian theology with the important phrase I-Thou as a
description of the personal relationship that should exist
between man and God. Early in his life, Buber had been
drawn to an aesthetic, inward, mystical type of religion.
Later, when he developed his description of the personal
as I-Thou encounter, he rejected mysticism. He never
allowed the I-Thou relationship to be called "mystical."
Whatever is "mystical" seemed to him to refer to a feeling
or a "something"—an "it"—*inside* the self. Whatever the
I-Thou relationship may be, it is certainly not a thing,
like a feeling, that is located inside the self. I-Thou is a
relationship that lies not inside but *between*. With this
starting point, it is easy to see how I-Thou theology
would come to the conclusion that whatever is personal
must exclude the mystical.

According to Buber, the world presents itself to man in
two ways—a personal way and an impersonal way. The
name of that which we experience impersonally is *it*.
Thou is the name addressed to a presence whom we
"meet" and whom we cannot, strictly speaking, "experience." A person met is not a thing experienced. Of
course, the person we meet may become an item of
experience. This depersonalizing of thou occurs when,
instead of direct address, we turn away and say "he" or
"she" and then discuss some aspect of the person's
appearance or character. When we say "he" or "she," we
are, in effect, saying "it." Whatever I observe, imagine,
feel, think, will, or use is a *something*, an *it*. I cannot
direct myself in any of these ways toward the Thou. If I

do, I objectify the Thou and make it into an "It," about which I entertain some purpose. The Thou simply presents itself to me by grace and is not the object of my action or seeking. No matter how spiritual the idea that I may entertain, if I "entertain" it, that idea is an It, not a Thou. "No purpose intervenes between I and Thou. . . . Only where all means have disintegrated encounters occur."[1] Whatever is an "it" is in the past. "It" is a thing that has happened. And whatever is an "it" is *my* object to act upon. The Thou meets me in the present. I and Thou enter into a relation of mutuality. I and Thou is a present happening, not a past event or "fact."

Buber's description of a personal relationship of I-Thou as distinguished from an impersonal relationship of I-It can be briefly indicated in outline:

I-It	I-Thou
The "It" is an object of experience.	The Thou is met.
The "It" is sought.	The Thou comes by grace.
An "It" is the object of my purpose (creative, noetic, or moral).	No purpose intervenes between I and Thou.
The "It" is in the past. A fact.	The Thou is encountered in the present.
I act upon "It." I am active. The "It" is passive.	I-Thou is a relation of reciprocity, mutual interaction.

When one thinks of the way the Christian mystics like Eckhart and Teresa describe their relationship with God, one encounters several difficulties in calling their sort of relation an "I-Thou" one. First, the mystic (preliminarily) actively seeks God, making him, in a way, an object or purpose and not a Thou. Second, the mutuality and reciprocity between I and Thou is sometimes denied in the mystics' relationship with God. According to Buber, the mystic emphasizes God's sovereignty and man's absolute dependence or creatureliness so as to *deactualize* man's contribution as a *partner* in the relationship.[2] Brunner's objection is just the opposite. The mystic seems to him to be the active seeker of God, who, as the one sought, is made a passive "It." The third difficulty is that the tendency in mystics like Eckhart to identify God and the soul means that God is not an *other* to whom one can say "Thou." Identity cannot be a relationship. This conviction is also characteristic of the devotional Hinduism, Bhakti. Recall the song of Tukaram, page 52.

We need to notice, however, that there is at least one important feature of I-Thou encounter that seems, despite Buber's disclaimer, to represent a mystical element. That is its unmediated nature. I and Thou come together in the *immediacy* of present time. While the I and the Thou do not, in a spatial sense, merge, some immediacy is nevertheless necessary for the relationship. Whatever I-Thou is, it is certainly not a discursive sorting of objects or ideas but, in some sense, a direct knowing. We need to return to this idea of immediacy.

Emil Brunner: The Mystical and the Personal Made Opposites

I-Thou encounter is given one of its most systematic Christian applications in the theology of Emil Brunner.[3] Mysticism was not at the center of Brunner's attention, but for a study of Christian mysticism Brunner is important in showing how a part of modern theology came to banish mysticism as a useful resource for theology. Brunner, along with neo-orthodoxy generally, found mysticism and the personal to be diametrically opposed.

Brunner was a Swiss pastor and professor of systematic theology at the University of Zurich. His early critique of Schleiermacher in *Die Mystik und Das Wort* directed his whole theology toward disengaging I-Thou personalism from mysticism. In 1934, in a famous "controversy" with Karl Barth, the main issue was the extent to which each was willing to grant the legitimacy of a *natural* as opposed to a *revealed* theology. Although Barth and Brunner differed on the details, both were concerned to put special stress on the *sola gratia* doctrine of their Protestant heritage. In doing so, they especially stressed the *discontinuity* of any pathway from man upwards to God.

Remembering St. Teresa's raptures or Meister Eckhart's paradoxes, one would naturally think that a preference for rational discontinuity could be called "mystical." Certainly it can and often is, but Brunner's usage is just the opposite. Brunner always interprets a "mystical" man-God relationship as one characterized by continuity. He thinks that for the mystic, man's knowledge of God is spun out of his own essential nature, like a spider spinning his thread. There needs to be a "break" wherever face-to-face encounter takes place. There must be "over-againstness" of I and Thou.

Brunner develops two ways of expressing the break that the I-Thou relationship requires.

The first way is to put reason on display in its state of brokenness. *Paradox* is made the essential expression of the personal relationship between man and God.

> We must have rational clarity and simplicity or paradox! . . . It would not be a divine revelation at all if it could be grasped by the mind, if it could be "perceived." . . . Revelation . . . cannot be anything other than illogical, since it breaks through the continuity of the human and natural sphere in general. . . .
>
> The continuity of thought must . . . be broken through. . . . So long as men believe that it is possible to know God apart from any special revelation, . . . they believe that He can be known in continuity with themselves (subjective Immanence); He is therefore regarded as a force which is continuous with the world (objective Immanence), as a mere Idea, not as a personality.[4]

Brunner's position is quite different from the classic modern interpreters Underhill, Inge, and von Hügel.

They wished to be rid of much of the irrationality of mysticism in order to employ the spiritual "laws" that they thought could be drawn from examples of mystical experience. That which they termed "true" and "humanizing" in the mystics' quest was precisely those things in continuity with man's rational endowments. Revelation was not discontinuous with these but a further development of them. It must not be said, however, that Brunner was antirationalist in the sense of one who can find no use for reason. The role he ascribed to reason was limited and critical. Reason functioned best, he thought, when it abandoned the illusion of rational autonomy. Revelation is "the meeting of two subjects, the divine and human." [5] It represents a breach of continuity and cannot be expressed by a principle of reason that will admit no breach.

The important thing to notice is that Brunner puts the mystic's quest in the same category with the rationalist's quest. "In the last resort, the God of Idealism . . . and of mysticism is always impersonal, because continuity exists between Him and the world, between Him and the Self." Mysticism and speculation differ, he said, only with respect to their method—ratiocination or the techniques of prayer. "In both instances it is the self-movement of man whose aim is God, whether it be through the soaring of thought or the introversion of the mystic. Both are in sharp contrast to the Christian faith, where the movement is on the side of God, and the aim is man." [6] Mysticism and speculation each attempts in its own way to traverse an unbroken "way" to God. For Brunner, such an attempt can never succeed in finding a personal God, who is not "found" but "encountered." Thus, Brunner's first way of trying to show the disruption of the man-God continuity is to employ paradox or broken reason. Paradox is the only way (and an indirect way, at that) by which the personal can be expressed by reason. Paradox is reason breaking under the impossible task of expressing the personal.

The second way of expressing the needed discontinuity is developed in Brunner's ethics. An ethic of rational continuity would be a casuistic ethic in which some moral principle is applied to the concrete case. Brunner throws out this type of ethic as quickly as he throws out any sort of rationalism. He looks to Kant's formal ethic to supply some clue for an ethic of discontinuity. Man lives under an absolute moral imperative. It is always true of man that he "ought." But Kant was wrong, Brunner believed, when he made the moral imperative something that man, in his rational capacity, addresses to himself. Brunner holds that it is man's nature to be addressed by God. Theologically considered, man is under a divine imperative. Man's sense of "responsibility," is, as the word implies, his "ability" to "respond" to a Thou addressed to him by God.

There is something important here for the consideration of the mystical and the personal as Brunner understands it. It is that Brunner, in developing his ethic, comes, at times, perilously close to the "distinterestedness of the mystics. If Brunner is to avoid rational continuity, he must avoid making the divine command a principle or regulation. Man's ethical life, he thinks, consists of *decision*. Decision is a "flying leap" rather than a "gliding motion." Decision is the ethical moment of rational discontinuity. Although man is under an absolute obligation of obedience, he does not thereby know precisely what action he ought to take. The command breaks in upon him and can never, on the basis of any immanent rational principle, be predicted by him.

> Hence I cannot know beforehand the content of the Command as I can know that of the Law. I can only receive it afresh each time through the voice of the Spirit.

> The particular decision is not anticipated; it cannot be "looked up" in the ethical law-book. The whole responsibility rests upon the individual himself; this kind of love alone is free from heteronomy, as well as from the self-glorification of autonomy. Therefore, in its external

appearance it is "opportunistic," "lacking in principles," while it too, and it alone, is free from all caprice. Each of its decisions is a "discovery," but each of such "discoveries"—if this love is true and real—is "something given." It is the end of the law, as it is also its fulfilment. [7]

The question arises as to whether this discontinuity in ethics means that, against his intentions, Brunner has approached the capriciousness of an Eckhartian disinterested love. And here again is an idea we need to return to. Is there mystical disinterestedness in I-Thou encounter?

When we ask what conditions Brunner requires in order to establish the personal, we may summarize them with the two phrases: rational discontinuity (expressed as paradox) and ethical discontinuity (expressed as decision and unmotivated love). Both moralism and mysticism, as Brunner sees them, assert "the continuity of human existence with the divine or with the absolute." [8] What is necessary to establish the personal, then, is a breach of continuity.

Brunner's whole theology can be viewed as an elucidation of the contrast he would make between the mystical type of religion on the one hand and the preferred, personal (Christian) type on the other. In Brunner's theology, we have an entirely *systematic* rejection of mysticism on the grounds that it is *impersonal*. Brunner's type of theology has left Protestantism in a much weakened position for a critical appreciation of mysticism. The reason is that Brunner regards mysticism as a *type* of religion to which he counterposes Christian faith as *personal*. If one follows Brunner, then to say "mystical" is tantamount to saying "impersonal" and thus "non-Christian." It is plain that his premises entail the utter rejection of any Christian mysticism.

Elements of Mysticism in I-Thou Encounter

Two things are wrong with this diametrical opposition between the personal and the mystical, the grounds for which will occupy us more fully in our discussion of immediacy.

The first objection is to Brunner's typological thinking, for it is this that dictates his either-or choice between the mystical and the personal. It is better, we suggest, to think of mysticism as a pattern composed of many elements, than as a monolithic structure which, if accepted, is completely controlling and which, if rejected, is rejected in its entirety. A critical view of mysticism allows us to select from mysticism those elements that might affirm the personal. On the confidence that there are such elements depends the whole value of Christian mysticism.

The second criticism points to the fact that some elements of mysticism do in fact appear in I-Thou encounter.

1. There can be no meeting between I and Thou except in the immediacy of the present. If mysticism is, as we have suggested, "the recovery or achievement of immediacy," then some element of mysticism has worked itself into I-Thou personalism despite all effort to avoid it. For a Christian theologian like Brunner, the question is how Christ "as an historical figure . . . is also the One who speaks to us in the intimacy of faith."[9] How, in other words, is the past made present? How does the past "fact" become a present "Thou"? Brunner's answer, developed more fully in his christological work *The Mediator,* shows how great is his reliance on paradox and how near he comes to mystical immediacy:

Complete immediacy in the midst of complete mediacy: this is the paradox of reconciliation, of justification, of faith. It is not that we can say that the Christian faith possesses a mystical aspect as well as an objective and historical aspect; this would be a very crude way of describing the situation. Here we are not concerned with connecting two essentially alien elements, nor even with an organic synthesis. However paradoxical it may sound to say so, the one is the other.[10]

Our question is why is it a "crude way" of describing the situation to say that the Christian faith possesses a mystical aspect as well as an historical aspect? Is that not, in fact, a more precise way of describing the situation?

2. To rely on paradox is to employ a device of mysticism. When that which one has to say cannot be said with words, then words break. Paradoxes do not directly convey meaning themselves; they point to a meaning derived from some other source. What is the other source? Of the possibilities here, Brunner suggests, rather than fully describes, two. First, the paradox may indicate some interior, hidden truth that has lain dormant within the self or nature and is now awakened by the stimulus of the paradox. The koan of Zen Buddhism, for example, is meant to awaken one to a hidden truth that had been there all along. This use of paradox Brunner firmly rejects. It directs one's attention to oneself and to that truth which is in continuity with oneself. It is subjective and fails to witness to a Thou that does not lie within but addresses one from without. [11] But Brunner means to use paradox to point to personal revelatory encounter. Paradox is the despair of rationality, which serves as the antechamber of faith. Ceasing to look to reason for the truth means, to Brunner, ceasing to look at oneself; for reason, as autonomous, he always regards as an extension of the self. His own paradoxes are intended to function as signposts that say, Dead End—Turn Another Way. He thinks the paradoxes of mysticism encourage rational perseverance. They are like signposts that say, Poor Visibility—Proceed With Care.

Despite Brunner's efforts, it is difficult and perhaps impossible to use paradox at all without pointing to something already present or known. If paradox points to the personal, this pointing will inform me only if the personal has already come into my experience. It need not mean that I *have* the personal latently or interiorly, but it does mean that at some point in my history I have already confronted the personal or am presently being confronted by it. The paradox would be a useless witness if its meaning were not already known or available to me *within* my present context. While Brunner avoids the interiority of the *individual,* he substitutes for it an interiority of the believing *community,* to which the paradox is understandable. The church may then be left addressing itself in paradoxes that only its believers have the experience to understand. Brunner does not altogether avoid all forms of immediacy and continuity and, therefore, he does not avoid a feature he himself regards as mystical.

3. The third element of mysticism that works into I-Thou theology is the denial of any instrumental means (things, "its") that intervene between the I and the Thou. Only the love without a reason, says Brunner, is real and personal. Otherwise, it is not a love of the person but a love of an idea. "The man who loves without conditions . . . does not allow his attitude to be determined by the attitude of the other. . . . He no longer loves him *'for* something,' but simply because he exists. That is what it means to love our neighbour." It is the "unrestricted recognition of the other man, without considering what he is like."[12]

At times the unmotivated nature of love is stressed to the point of depriving the community of a way of discriminating and assessing priorities for service. "Your neighbour is the person who meets you. In the 'Calling' your neighbour is given to you; you do not need to hunt for him, therefore you do not need to search for the sphere of service. It is not for *us* to choose the tasks which God has thought out and destined for us."[13]

Nor is it permissible for a moral evaluation of the neighbor to be allowed to be a motive. That the neighbor is possessed of a rightous or unrighteous will should not have the least effect on love. If love took into consideration such moral facts as these, it would lose its innocent—unmotivated—character. This character can only be maintained by "the irrational nature of love."[14]

We can see that no *reason,* no motive for love can be tolerated—not even the motive of another's moral excellence and lovableness; for to love out of consideration for moral excellence is still to have a *motive* and means that an idea or "thing" is what is loved, rather than the person himself. In these conceptions, I-Thou theology certainly approaches the disinterested love of the mystics.

The tinge of mysticism in I-Thou theology raises the question of whether it is possible or even desirable to write theology with an eye to expunging from it all mysticism. Must the choice be the mystical or the personal? Such a choice seems dictated by strict typological thinking in the first place. Mysticism is less a monolith than a reservoir. Not everything in it is a help to the personal, but neither is everything in it a denial of the personal. Moreover, some mystical elements find their way into that theology which struggles hardest to express the personal: (1) I-Thou encounter requires an immediacy of present time; (2) its reliance on paradox requires an immediacy of knowing and a denial of discursus and proof; (3) I-Thou encounter also requires immediacy in the sense of a spontaneous, unmotivated act. We find that I-Thou personalism, like mysticism, attempts to recover immediacy in some sense. Just what is meant by immediacy requires closer attention.

The Mystical, the Personal, and the Meanings of Immediacy

Throughout the preceding chapters, we have tried to show how mysticism is in some sense the "recovery of immediacy." We can now say that the I-Thou relation is also, in some sense, a recovery of immediacy and that, accordingly, it adopts elements of mysticism. But it is not simple to say what immediacy is and how it might be recovered. Im-mediacy means "a denial of something which comes between." But *what* is it that might come between? And between what two things does it come? Here we consider three meanings of *immediacy* that are derived from the kind of intervening thing that immediacy denies. First, immediacy as a spatial expression denies separation or distance. The words "at one," "within," or "identical" express its meaning. I-Thou theology vigorously rejects immediacy in this spatial sense and most strongly dissociates itself from mysticism at this point. Second, immediacy as a temporal expression denies an interval of time. The words "present" or "presence" express its meaning. The I-Thou relationship needs immediacy in this sense and opens itself here to the mystical. Third, immediacy as a spontaneous act is the denial of some intervening technical operation or means. The technical operation that is denied may be (a) rational discursus or proof. In the case of immediacy of knowing, for example, no rational process may intervene between the knower and that which he knows. The denied technical operation may be (b) some ethical purpose, motive, or principle that intervenes between the agent and his act. Unmotivated or spontaneous love would be an example. I-Thou theology makes use of spontaneous immediacy in both its epistemological and ethical applications.

Immediacy as a Spatial Expression: The Denial of Separation. Distance, or "space between," is what is denied in that sense of immediacy which makes use of the metaphor of space. In the mystical idea of ascent or pilgrimage, the nearness or "immediacy" of God is made ultimately more vivid by exaggerating the *preliminary* distance. The immediacy of God is depicted architecturally, for example, by showing an enormous distance that is overcome as one approaches the holy place.[15] The approach to the great Buddha of Kamakura awakens a sense of presence in the pilgrim who traverses the distance. A great cathedral makes the same declaration. Notre Dame of Paris, visible from a great distance, represents the end of some spiritual quest. The one who approaches must climb steps and enter large doors. There he is faced with yet another prospect, the long nave. Only ultimately does he climb the chancel steps and approach the altar. The pilgrim at Our Lady of Guadalupe in Monterrey, who crawls along a path for miles on his knees simply to approach the church edifice itself, dramatizes the *ultimate* immediacy of God by overcoming the great distance between himself and God. The one whose journey has been long is all the more enfolded in a welcoming embrace.

In the case of the speculative mystics, the preliminary distance between man and God is emphasized as a *via negativa*. Conceptually, God is "located" a great distance from our common ways of thinking. "Unto this darkness which is beyond Light we pray that we may come." The mysteriousness of God is the conceptual "distance" that lies between man and God. "Essence alone satisfies and God keeps on withdrawing farther and farther away, to arouse the mind's zeal and lure it on to follow and finally to grasp the true good that has no cause."[16]

When the pilgrim reaches his goal after overcoming a great distance, he depicts the reunion as a total absence of distance—as identity or merging. The pilgrim is ultimately absorbed in God like a drop of water in a sponge, as St. Teresa managed to say it. God is in me like a "spark" within my soul, said Eckhart. "God's is-ness (*istigkeit*) is my is-ness." Now, at last, the pilgrim knows God in the immediacy of communion. Yet, paradoxically, he cannot speak of God, or else he reintroduces the distance he has now overcome. "How," asks Plotinus, "can we represent as different from us that which did not seem, while we were contemplating it, not other than ourselves but in perfect at-oneness with us?" "The knower and the known are one," said Eckhart. "Simple people imagine that they should see God, as if He stood there and they here. This is not so. God and I, we are one in knowledge."[17]

The overcoming of the distance may be described with such words as "within" or "identical." Deification of the soul, or the identification of the soul and God, is not an act of self-worship—at least certainly not in intention. It is a denial of a perceivable difference between the self and God: "My Me is God, nor do I recognize any other Me except my God Himself." "To gauge the soul we must gauge it with God, for the Ground of God and the Ground of the Soul are one and the same."[18] The charge of subjectivism against the mystics is often too crudely drawn. The prior question is whether there is a pure subjectivity any more than there is a pure objectivity. Self-awareness is not the enclosure of the self in its private world. Even Feuerbach's subjectivism was not a crude self-worship but the worship of humanity (addressed as "Thou") exalted to a divine degree. I-Thou theology accepts some forms of immediacy, but the meaning of immediacy it most vigorously and successfully opposes is immediacy expressed in spatial metaphors like *within* or *identical*. These spatial metaphors seem to depersonalize the man-God relationship. No doubt the mystics often took their spatial metaphors too literally. But if I-Thou theology, in the interest of the personal, asks that introspection and subjectivity be eliminated, it asks for something that is as undesirable as it is impossible to fulfill. And like mysticism itself, it then makes too literal and spatial the distinction between what is without and what is within—rejecting the within. Self-knowledge is as much conferred by a social context as is the ability to say "thou." Introspection need not mean that one is encapsulated in a private world. Introspection may rather be the avenue through which one learns to say "thou" and to attend with sympathy to the feelings of another.

Immediacy as a Temporal Expression: The Denial of a Time Interval. Immediacy in another sense is a temporal metaphor. If one says "immediate" in a literal sense, one may mean only that two events occur at the same time or without a noticeable interval. With a stop watch, one could measure the time interval between two events, and if there were no elapsed time, the second event would be said to be "simultaneous" with the first or to follow it "immediately." But this is hardly the mystics' meaning when they, like Eckhart, speak of an "Eternal Now." Nor

is it the meaning of "presence" in I-Thou encounter.
What is denied by the temporal metaphor is not a literal
interval of time. What is denied is the applicability of
time and its passing. "Eternal Now," "eternity," "presence" and those words that St. Teresa loved to pro-
nounce—"forever-ever-ever"—show that immediacy
denies the appropriateness of time. *Immediacy,* for both
I-Thou theology and mysticism, means an inherently
immeasurable "now," a present or presence in which two
subjects, I and Thou, are delivered to each other "all at
once." Buber pointed out that, in the case of man, all
moments of presence become past events. When one
says "he" or "she" instead of "thou," one places in the
past what was once a living presence. But when one
thinks of God addressing man as "thou," one cannot
think that the past would ever overtake the "eternal now"
in which God speaks. Only that which is both personal
and holy can make its presence permanently accessible.
God as the Eternal Now is not a timeless God permanently at rest, but a holy, personal God permanently
accessible, or "present." Man has a presence that he
carries with him always and through which he, from
time to time, opens himself to others. This presence is his
best analogue of God's "timelessness and eternity." It is
true that the more theoretical and the less experiential
and practical the mystics were, the more likely they were
to make the now of God literally timeless. Given the
inheritance of Plato and Aristotle, it was difficult to stop
short of a conception of God as a changeless *actus purus.*
Yet the theorizing of the speculative mystics was done
for the sake of something else—an immediate, lively, and
practical apprehension of God as being. Immediacy of
the man-God relation need not mean a literal timelessness. It need only mean that God is such a one that
wherever man is or whatever his condition, God is
present to him. The timeless now of God is his universal
accessibility and presence.

The Christian's special embarrassment in thinking of
immediacy as "present" is that his Scripture speaks of

things that are past. Facts lie in the past. Are facts nonessential to an immediate, personal relationship with God? It is always the mystic's tendency to de-emphasize the importance of past facts out of consideration for a living presence. The Bible itself has something to contribute to this preference for the present. There is certainly a universalizing strand in the Bible, as well as a factual and ethical strand. Jesus, interpreted as the Logos, is made available beyond the limits of Nazareth and beyond the limits of the first century. He is present, not simply past. But total disengagement from the past—from facts, from externals and "its"—amounts to a special temptation for the Christian. Baron von Hügel was full of scolding advice to Evelyn Underhill for making externals "mere" externals. Even St. Teresa warned her nuns not to count the "Sacred Humanity of Christ" among the "objects" from which they should withdraw. To do so is "to walk on air."[19] It is Christianity's stake in what happened in the past that restrains the Christian theologian from simply converting the past into the present. To the Christian theologian, mysticism is therefore always suspect. Some of the schools of Hinduism and Buddhism can more easily de-emphasize the past in favor of immediacy and timelessness. Buddha essence can easily supplant the historical Buddha. Christianity, which can never entirely suppress the question *Did it happen?* has a less easy relationship with mysticism.

Nevertheless, insofar as Christianity celebrates a presence, it admits into itself an element of mysticism even if it calls that presence "Thou." It is as difficult for I-Thou theology to make use of the past as it is for mysticism. Both prefer the present. We can discern no essential difference between the mystic's use of temporal immediacy and the I-Thou use.

Immediacy Expressed as a Spontaneous Act: The Denial of an Intervening Technique. Immediacy in another sense expresses how something is done. Immediacy, when it applies to doing something—whether that something is (a) an act of knowing or (b) a moral act—is the *spontaneity* of the act. Here what is denied by the word "immediacy" is the technique "by which" a thing is known or done. Immediacy of knowing is a denial of the need for an intervening proof that comes "between" the one who knows and that which he knows. When immediacy is applied to a moral act, it means that no rationale, no "purpose," no motive intervenes between the one who acts and the act itself. His act simply flows from him "spontaneously." The best way to pray, said St. Teresa, is for the prayer to flow simply from the heart like rain falling from heaven. No effort, no technique intervenes between the one who prays and the prayer that he prays. St. Teresa's gradations in prayer are, in fact, the step-by-step removal of all technical means of praying so that, finally, the prayer itself springs from the heart "immediately."

(a) Immediacy of Knowing. When immediacy in this nontechnical sense is applied to the way of knowing, all evidence and proofs, all means of verification, are rejected. Certainly, the I-Thou relationship is dependent on immediacy in this sense. Immediacy of knowing is also the ultimate aim of the mystics—however occupied they are preliminarily with techniques. Plotinus deemed *Nous,* the immediate kind of knowing, superior to discursive reason (*dianoia* and *epistēmē*), which occupied itself with sorting through the means of knowing. Zen Buddhism, in the most paradoxical fashion, uses a technique that is designed to "self-destruct" as soon as it is used: the koan is the inherently unsolvable puzzle that brings to an abrupt halt all techniques and means in the act of knowing. Immediacy of knowing can offer no means "by which" to certify itself. Mysticism, whose ultimate aim is immediacy of knowing, is therefore understandably often called "irrational."

In philosophical idealism and mysticism, immediacy of knowing has often been a most highly prized way of knowing. Its validation derives from nothing outside itself and, therefore, takes second place to nothing.

Whatever has to come with its "reasons in its hands," as Nietzsche complained of Socrates, comes, as it were, flawed by the need to justify itself. The one like Raskolnikov in *Crime and Punishment,* who goes repeatedly to the police to "explain" himself and ask to be interrogated, begins to raise suspicions. That which is most real and most true ought to be manifestly persuasive in and of itself, without anything outside mediating its authenticity. It should produce its own authentication at the moment it manifests itself. Such is the mystic's strongest conviction.

Especially does it seem to the mystic and to the idealist that man's knowledge of God ought to be unmediated by any technical means. God, as *a se,* as self-sufficient, should not be dependent on any validating reason other than God himself. This line of thinking, called the Platonist-Augustinian strand in Western religious thought culminates in Descartes. It is the kind of consideration that led Anselm to his Ontological Argument. He began with a search for "a single argument which would require no other for its proof than itself alone."[20] For Anselm the idea of "a being than which nothing greater can be conceived" was the self-authenticating idea. Clearly, Anselm thought that a single proof is better than a string of proofs because the single proof removes as much as possible the technical means of knowing. Every rejection of an evidentiary means—whether the rejection is expressed by a concept of perfection (Anselm), a feeling of absolute dependence (Schleiermacher), creature feeling (Otto), or the revelatory Thou (Buber, neo-orthodoxy)—is an attempt to make manifest the God who is self-authenticating. Certainly I-Thou theology is in full alliance with mysticism in rejecting evidentiary means. Paradox, both in mysticism and I-Thou theology, declares the rejection of means.

Another line of thinking, labeled the Aristotelian-Thomistic strand, sees that whatever makes a bid to be believed must submit to some criterion of judgment.

Untrustworthy as our judgments are, we need to have
some means "by which" to test them. Ideas come into
man from outside him, from the sensory world. They do
not immediately produce themselves within him. These
ideas need to be sorted out and arranged by means of the
rational procedures of discursive reason. When these
procedures are carried out correctly, the end result is
sound. Aquinas' various cosmological proofs are just
such an attempt. God is not known in immediacy. Such
knowledge as we have of him, derived as it is from the
imperfect sensory world, is incomplete. But of that *part*
we do have we can be sure, since we can review the
means "by which" it is authenticated. Furthermore, its
validity is not a private matter but is open to all who will
take the trouble to review the argument. Knowledge of
God, however, must wait upon such a review. It is *a
posteriori* and does not come immediately, before (*a
priori*) the evidence is considered. Of course, neither the
a priori arguments of Anselm nor the *a posteriori*
arguments of Thomas Aquinas are valid arguments for
the existence of God. They serve as symbols of a
theological dilemma: (a) immediate knowledge in which
God is known wholly, yet which knowledge cannot be
defended publicly by means of available evidence and (b)
knowledge of God that is second best (i.e., derived from
other kinds of knowledge) but available to all who will
examine the means of its acquisition. *Ultimately*, the
mystic seeks immediate knowledge, as in (a), in which
he rejects all means of knowing. But *preliminarily,* the
mystic can, as in (b), make use of some means of
knowing such as experience or rational discursus.

Because the mystic's ultimate aim is immediacy of
knowing, he can furnish no "proof" or evidence. But as
we have often said throughout these chapters, the mystic
has a *preliminary* concern as well as an *ultimate* aim. He
is one who is learning and teaching how to do
something—how to pray, how to think of God. When the
mystic needs to make his knowledge available to others,
he can do so only by putting into the hands of someone

else the *means* by which he came by his knowledge. For all his ultimate denials of technical means, he does have a preliminary technique to teach. The guru, the Zen master, the Christian novice mistress are occupied with teaching an apprentice how to do something. This is what is meant by calling the mystics' preliminary stage "practical." Preliminarily, they are much occupied with means, however emphatic may be their ultimate denials of means. What the mystic teaches, though drawn from experience, is not a general conclusion derived from scientifically discrete empirical procedures. He teaches, rather, a skill which he himself has learned through his community and its traditional wisdom. Certainly when St. Teresa says that she teaches what she has learned by "great experience" she means "experience" in something like the German sense of *Erfahren* rather than *Erlebnis*—not the practice of an exact science, but an art learned by a lifetime of spiritual groping.[21] The word "experience" in mysticism is used in its broadest sense. If "truth" applies only to what experience in some statistically significant sense shows, then the mystic can make no claims to access to it. His techniques, though derived from "experience"—and even sometimes called "experimental"—are not directed toward public verifiability. The mystic, on his knees in prayer, does not acquire new facts about the empirical world, nor is that his aim.[22] Certainly, he throws himself on his knees because of his estimate of the nature and value of the empirical world when measured against a "that world." But nothing hc does or says will make *publicly* valid any truth he discerns there. He can only say to the apprentice, from out of his own experience, "Go along this path." I-Thou personalism, like mysticism in its ultimate stage, rejects all evidentiary means of knowing. But the I-Thou relation appears to have no preliminary stage that accepts technical means and which can therefore say, "Go along this path." Mysticism thus makes some room for "its"—the "thing element" in religion—in a way that I-Thou cannot.[23]

(b) Immediacy in Ethics. In ethics, the denial of all means and technique implies a purely spontaneous act. Like immediacy of knowing, immediate *goodness*, which is to say "innocence," is highly prized. It is that goodness that issues forth seemingly without the employment of any technique. Much of the charm of the Tao-Te Ching derives from the effortless spontaneity that is described there. The spontaneous act is not, strictly speaking, a moral act. To say that an act is "moral" implies that one has taken thought about it. Some determination of the will, some purpose or reason, intervenes between the agent and his act. Some agonizing always attends the question, Should I or shouldn't I? If one were really in "harmony" with goodness (as the Taoists put it), then one's act of goodness would spring from oneself effortlessly and spontaneously.

Much in the world's scripture suggests that the "best" sort of act is not in the exact sense "good" or "just." It is not the act that arises from some prior determination of what is good and what is just; it is an outflow of natural goodness or innocence that springs spontaneously from the self.

> The act of sacred duty,
> Done without attachment,
> Not as pleasure desired,
> Not as hated compulsion,
> By him who has no care
> For the fruit of his action:
> That act is of sattwa.[24]

> It was when the Great Way declined
> That human kindness and morality arose;
> It was when intelligence and knowledge appeared
> That the Great Artifice began.[25]

And which of you by being anxious can add one cubit to his span of life? (Matthew 6:27)

Any taking thought about a deed to be done is, to the mystic's mind, a deed of less purity than the act that simply flows from the self. "Do all you do, acting from the core of your soul, without a single 'Why'" (Eckhart). Sincerity, naturalness, the absence of duplicity and self-interest—these are the ways we describe such an act. One also, when one speaks of personal encounter, denies intervening moral judgments. Encounter is a happening in the context of mutual acceptance—a nonjudgmental climate. It is not something one tries to do by some *means*. "Only where all means have disintegrated encounters occur" (Buber). The mystic sees that the most excellent moral state is not morality at all but an innocence that transcends the distinction between good and evil. His ultimate aim is the recovery of that moral immediacy which is innocence. He wishes to return to "the womb from which I came," where "what I wanted, I was and what I was, I wanted" (Eckhart).

No doubt spontaneity in moral life is a vision of an ideal state, not a practical program. I-Thou encounter can take place only in the absence of anything that compels or judges. Mystical detachment is, likewise, the absence of decisiveness and moral effort. Yet equally for mysticism and I-Thou encounter, it can be dangerous to make a practical program out of innocence. Such things as episodes of debauchery in Russian monasticism or the crimes of the California Manson family of 1970, are conscious attempts to pass beyond good and evil through immoral or criminal acts "spontaneously" and "innocently" performed. At the very least, if one makes spontaneity into a practical ethical program, one forfeits all tactics, pressure, and lobbying in the sphere of practical politics. And, in personal ethics, when one relinquishes resolve and means in favor of sincerity, one may relinquish the act altogether. Sincerity that flows from the heart can disappear as spontaneously as it appears.[26]

Mysticism: A Pattern, Not a Type

To understand mysticism as a type of religious orientation in diametrical opposition to the personal is to

misrepresent it. As a world view, mysticism sees a
distinction between "this world" and "that world"—
however it may describe the two. "That world" may
simply be a deeper conception of "this world"—the Tao
or the "way." "That world" may be called Brahman, God,
or Heaven. How is the mystic to recover "that world"?
The means may be an arduous spiritual journey or
simply "seeing," or satori. The mystic may speak more
fully about *the way* to achieve his end. Or he may be
more concerned with the end itself. St. Teresa gives
more detailed instruction about the mystic's *way,*
whereas the Taoists advise us only to be natural. In any
event, mysticism begins with a separation, whether
radical or only apparent, between two worlds, and it
seeks to bind them together again.

Mysticism is thus a pattern in two aspects. Preliminarily, it asks how to make use of "this world" in order to
rejoin "that world." Ultimately, mysticism is passive,
ineffable, and otherworldly. Is mysticism irrational? If we
confine what is rational to this-worldly discursus,
mysticism is surely ultimately irrational. It is not strictly
(only broadly and preliminarily) empirical. Furthermore,
it discerns levels of reason, and non-discursive reason
passes beyond the level of the sayable. Whether what is
unsayable ought to be called "irrational," we leave to the
refinements of philosophical debate. Yet, "unsayable-
ness"—mystery—is a common experience. While it may
be irrational in the sense of noncognitive, it cannot be
irrational in the sense of odd or bizarre. The classic
interpreters of mysticism were right, we think, to
determine the value of mysticism by what it offered all
men. Is mysticism otherworldly and passive? Preliminarily, no. Ultimately, yes. Yet, paradoxically, the
otherworldly vision prompts a disposition to reform:
Nothing in "this world" is so hallowed that it cannot be
discarded in favor of a higher vision. Is mysticism
depersonalizing? If the I-Thou relationship is taken as
the best analogue of the personal, mysticism is impersonal only when its metaphors of immediacy are taken

too literally and too spatially. But if a personal relationship requires intimacy and encounter, the mystics know
well how to say "Thou."

Meditation on the Recovery of Immediacy

"We are embarked," said Pascal. From the moment of
birth, from the moment of self-awareness, of responsibility and articulateness, man, whether he acknowledges it
or not, is embarked. What can I know? What ought I to
do? What may I hope? These are the questions that have
stirred the philosophical spirit. Kant's response was to
write a critique that happens to make hard reading. In
that mythical time of original innocence (*illud tempus*,
Eliade calls it), "before," "back in the womb," man does
not ask such questions and does not need to ask. Purely
natural is all he need be. "It was when intelligence and
knowledge appeared that the Great Artifice began." To
speak, to think conceptually—these are the things we do
when we depart from innocence. Words, deeds and the
strain we put upon them, the search for the "truth" and
for the "good"—these are signs of our separation from
our mythic origin. If we write a critique or chant the Te
Deum or fight manfully for the right, if we emblazon a
canvas with color or dispense a motherly hug, we give a
signal of our debarkation from innocence and immediacy. There are needs existent in the world!—all signs of
our being embarked. As long as there is a need for
philosophical inquiry, the truth is not yet at hand; as long
as there is need to work for the right, justice does not
prevail; as long as it takes effort to express beauty, beauty
does not yet abound; as long as wounds need to be
healed, health is yet to come. It is not true, as Sartre's
Roquetin would have it, that we are nowhere and reeling
with *nausea*; we are between. But no one can live
between without asking, Where to?

The mystic lives out his voyage emboldened, consoled,
reassured, and delighted by his present vision of that
"whither." All men, being voyagers, are all, very nearly,
mystics. Even before his arrival, the mystic anticipates

and celebrates his destination. He has a future that has already begun to be present. It is true that he is something of an improvident fool. Careless of prudence, he spends his future now, so sure is he of its bounty—is he not presently enjoying it? Those who out of prudence refuse the taste of their destiny will suffer needless impoverishment of joy; there will be no "hallowing" of their "everyday." But if the mystic, in his celebration, altogether forgets that he is still en route and not yet arrived, he will be altogether a fool. He had better not have mysticism as the *whole* of his religion. Few mystics, in fact, were wholly mystics and nothing whatever else. What they see by their vision needs to be seen, as well, through the sightings and measurings of a practical, critical eye. But there is a self-correcting dynamic in the mystic's vision; he will not intentionally deceive himself. His overwhelming dissatisfaction with half-truth and veiled truth is born of his vision of a perfectly revealed truth.

In England, in a convent of contemplative nuns, the mother superior, Mother Mary Columba, once addressed herself to a question meant to be probing and testing. "Why would anyone closet herself like this, forsaking a life in the outside world?" Her answer? It came with the assurance of one who knew. "I think you only come to a place like this because you can't help it."

Not every mystical impulse leads to such a specialized life. Monasticism is not the same as mysticism. But "You can't help it" is still the answer to why anyone would attend to the mystical. Mysticism as a world view and a practice is born of our human condition—of *all* men's condition. We are embarked.

What is it that anyone stands to gain through his mystical apprehension? Simply put, it is the recovery of immediacy—immediacy of *time,* of *space,* and of *manner.* First, he gains something present that otherwise is delayed or absent. He claims the right to a present celebration that no awaiting and no planning can deliver to him *now.* Second, he gains something *here* that otherwise is *there*: a surety about himself, his identity and kinship with the holy. He gains a divinity that is as near to him as his own breath, one to whom he turns as readily as he turns to himself. Third, he gains something that accepts and restores him—without his earning that acceptance and restoration. He gains a reality, the knowledge of which does not await proof (to the logician a pity, to the supplicant a joy). He gains a "duty" to perform that flows spontaneously from a generous nature, a duty that knows no constraint of "ought." In a word, the mystic is given the ability to recover immediacy in its several forms. He who takes notice of his being embarked is already an incipient mystic. Far from being foreign to the human condition, mysticism arises from it. Mysticism had better not be the whole of one's religion, but the one who knows of his embarkation and senses the presence of his destination will have within his religion an element of the mystical.

Notes

Chapter 1

1. Leon S. Otis, *Psychology Today,* April 1974, p. 45.
2. *New York Times Magazine,* 26 January 1975, p. 12.
3. Ernst Troeltsch, *The Social Teaching of the Christian Churches* (New York: The Macmillan Co., 1931), II, 693.
4. Malcolm Muggeridge, *Jesus Rediscovered* (Garden City, N.Y.: Doubleday & Co., 1969), p. 112.
5. Ibid., pp. 115-16.
6. John Herman Randall, Jr., *The Role of Knowledge in Western Religion* (Boston: Star King Press, 1958), p. 15.
7. Sam Keen, *Apology for Wonder* (New York: Harper & Row, 1969), p. 119.
8. Harvey Cox, *Feast of Fools* (Cambridge: Harvard University Press, 1969), p. 114.
9. Ibid., p. 115.
10. *Newsweek,* 30 December, 1968, p. 39.
11. Quoted in John Hick, ed., *The Existence of God* (New York: The Macmillan Co., 1964), pp. 221-22.
12. E. S. Brightman, *A Philosophy of Religion* (New York: Prentice-Hall, 1940), p. 350. "A person," says E. S. Brightman, "is a self that is potentially self-conscious, rational and ideal. That is to say, when a self is able at times to reflect on itself as a self, to reason, and to acknowledge ideal goals by which it can judge its actual achievements, then, we call it a person."
13. Hick, *Existence of God,* pp. 178-79.
14. Evelyn Underhill, *Mysticism* (New York: Meridian Books, World Publishing Co., 1955), p. 24.
15. Troeltsch, *Social Teaching,* II, 693.
16. Olive Wyon, *The School of Prayer* (New York: The Macmillan Co., 1963), p. 6.
17. "It is a matter of common knowledge that Luther himself was greatly influenced by [mysticism]. Calvin, however, came far less under its influence. His doctrine of the Eucharist, too, does not agree with it, but rather with anti-Catholicism, and with the

tendency to place a great gulf between the Creator and the creature. Calvinism is related to the sect-type, but not to mysticism. In spite of that, however, mysticism penetrated into it" (Troeltsch, *Social Teaching*, II, 730).

18. William James, *The Varieties of Religious Experience* (New York: Collier Books, 1961), p. 59.

19. To be sure, the assumed content has implications for the type of relationship. In the words of Nicol Macnicol, "The goal of all mysticism is the same, namely the 'unitive' life, but its conception of that goal and of the path to it is largely influenced by its thought of that form which it seeks to escape, whether sin or *samsara*." We might add that it is also influenced by the nature of that with which it envisions union. See *Hastings Enclyclopedia of Religion and Ethics*, s.v. "Mysticism" (Hindu).

20. Whether the actual religious life of primitive peoples is in fact altogether characterized by such innocence is certainly open to question. See Paul Radin, *Primitive Man as a Philosopher*, and Bronislaw Malinowski, *Magic, Science, and Religion*.

21. Baron Friedrich von Hügel, "Commentary on the Idea of Deification in Pseudo-Dionysus," in *Eternal Life* (Edinburgh: T & T Clark, 1912), p. 100.

22. It is true, however, that as a kind of by-product of his vision, the mystic has frequently been engaged in social service. It is also true that mysticism has been historically linked with a spirit of reform especially in church practice and doctrine. How mysticism can add an impetus to reform without having reform as its primary aim is discussed below and is a theme of special interest in William E. Hocking's view of mysticism.

Chapter 2

1. William Theodore De Bary et al., comps., *Sources of Indian Tradition* (New York: Columbia University Press, 1958), p. 644.

2. Reflection on the Upanishads gave rise to six orthodox systems of philosophy. It is helpful to consider them in pairs:

    (1) Sankyha figures prominently in the Bhagavad-Gita. It is dualistic and atheistic. The two principle realities are purusha (spirit) and prakriti (matter). (2) Yoga is a similarly dualistic system, which, however, is theistic.

    (3) Mimamsa (which is action, or Karma-investigating, is called Karma Mimamsa and also Purva (Earlier) Mimamsa. It focuses on legal and ethical questions. (4) Vedanta (which is also called Uttara Mimamsa, or Later Mimamsa) is Brahma-investigating. In this prominent school there were several different emphases: Advaita Vedanta of Shankara (A.D. 850) held to a strict nondualism. The school of Ramanuja (*ca.* A.D. 1137) held to a qualified nondualism. The school of Madhva (A.D. 1199–1278) had a more theistic and pluralistic interpretation.

    (5) Vaisheshika was interested in the physical universe and was pluralistic. (6) Nyaya, likewise, was pluralistic but was more directed toward logic and methods of knowing than to physics.

3. In the Hindu analysis, man's actual aims in life are four. There is (1) kama, or pleasure, including sensual pleasure and aesthetic

cultivation; (2) artha, or business and worldly success; (3) dharma, or religious and moral duty, including the duty of each caste (Brahman, priestly; Kshatriya, soldierly, administrative; Vaishya, agricultural, productive; Sudra, laboring); and (4) moksha, or spiritual liberation and release.

Hindu appreciation for the variety in human nature is further emphasized by the four pathways it prescribes for different temperaments: (1) jnana-yoga, the way (or marga) of knowledge and discrimination; (2) bhakti-yoga, the way of devotion; (3) karma-yoga, the way of deeds, action, duty, and (4) raja-yoga, the classic way of meditation.

4. De Bary, *Sources of Indian Tradition*, p. 11.

5. Ibid., p. 9.

6. Surenda Nath Dasgupta, *Hindu Mysticism* (New York: Frederick Ungar Publishing Co., 1959), p. 9.

7. De Bary, *Sources of Indian Tradition*, p. 34.

8. Ibid., p. 35.

9. Heinrich Zimmer, *Philosophies of India* (New York: Meridian Books, World Publishing Co., 1958), p. 418.

10. Swami Prabhavananda and Christopher Isherwood, eds., *The Song of God: Bhagavad-Gita* (New York: Mentor Books, New American Library, 1944), p. 84.

11. Ibid., p. 129.

12. (1) Sattwa, the principle of purity and refinement; (2) rajas, the principle of action and passion; (3) tamas, the principle of solidity, resistance, and dullness. The principles describe such diverse things as temperaments of mind, the seasoning and relative refinement of foods, and the duty of the caste (Kshatrya is predominantly rajas). All three gunas are present in everything, but one predominates and gives that thing its character.

13. Quoted in Huston Smith, *The Religions of Man* (New York: Harper & Row, 1965), pp. 40-41.

14. Quoted in Kenneth W. Morgan, ed., *The Path of the Buddha* (New York: The Ronald Press, 1956), p. 22.

15. Quoted in Clarence H. Hamilton, ed., *Buddhism: A Religion of Infinite Compassion* (New York: The Liberal Arts Press, 1952), p. 5.

16. Quoted in Huston Smith, *Religions of Man*, p. 90.

17. Interpretations are drawn from Morgan, *Path of the Buddha*.

18. Yama, the killing of desire; niyama, self-discipline, calm, cleanliness; asana, position of the body; pranayama, breath regulation; pratyahara, withdrawal of the senses; dharana, concentration upon one thing; dhyana, half-conscious meditation; and samadhi, trance. See Mircea Eliade, "Yoga Technique in Buddhism," in *Yoga: Immortality and Freedom* (Princeton University Press, 1969) and Edward Conze, *Buddhist Meditations* (New York: The Macmillan Co., 1956).

19. De Bary, *Sources of Indian Tradition*, p. 107.

20. Thus L. de la Vallee Poussin and E. J. Thomas in *Hastings Encyclopedia of Religion and Ethics*, s.v. "Mysticism" (Buddhist): "There is no mysticism in Buddhism, if the word 'mysticism' is understood quite strictly: Immediate, non-discursive intuitive

relation with the Absolute." William Barrett and D. T. Suzuki find that Zen Buddhism, because of the absence of dualism between "lower and higher worlds," is "not mysticism as the West understands mysticism" (*Zen Buddhism: Selected Writings of D. T. Suzuki*, ed. William Barrett [Garden City, N.Y.: Doubleday Anchor Books, 1956], p. xvii).

21. Hamilton, *Buddhism: A Religion of Infinite Compassion*, pp. 124-25.
22. Arthur Waley, *The Way and Its Power: A Study of the Tao Tê Ching and Its Place in Chinese Thought* (New York: Grove Press, 1951), p. 151.
23. William Theodore De Bary et al., *Sources of Chinese Tradition* (New York: Columbia University Press, 1960), p. 50.
24. Ibid., p. 53.
25. Ibid., p. 57.
26. Ibid., p. 72; see also Arthur Waley, *Three Ways of Thought in Ancient China* (Garden City, N. Y.: Doubleday Anchor, 1956), p. 11.
27. Waley, *Three Ways of Thought*, p. 36.
28. Ibid., pp. 13-14.
29. Sören Kierkegaard, *Concluding Unscientific Postscript*, trans. David F. Swenson and Walter Lowrie (Princeton: Princeton University Press, 1944), p. 174.
30. Arthur Waley, *Three Ways of Thought*, pp. 36, 50.
31. Suzuki, *Zen Buddhism*, p. 88. See especially chap. 4, "Satori or Enlightenment" and chap. 6, "The Reason of Unreason: The Koan Exercise."
32. Ibid., pp. 134-35.
33. William Theodore De Bary, "A Visit to Eihei-ji" in *The Columbia Forum*, III, 32-38.
34. Ibid.
35. Adapted from Heinrich Zimmer, *Philosophies of India*, pp. 5-8.

Chapter 3

1. Sam Keen, *Apology for Wonder* (New York: Harper & Row, 1969), p. 79.
2. Raymond B. Blakney, trans., *Meister Eckhart* (New York: Harper & Brothers, 1941), pp. 99-100.
3. Ibid., p. 101. Meister Eckhart cites this passage in one of his sermons and interprets it, in true mystic's fashion, as an example of the deification of the soul.
4. William Ralph Inge, *Christian Mysticism* (London: Methuen & Co., 1948), pp. 45-48.
5. See chaps. 16–23, *The Cloud of Unknowing*, trans. Clifton Wolters (Baltimore: Penguin Books, 1971), pp. 73-83.
6. Franz Cumont, *Oriental Religions in Roman Paganism* (New York: Dover Publications, 1956), pp. 44-45.
7. Rudolf Bultmann, *Primitive Christianity* (New York: Meridian Books, World Publishing Co., 1956), p. 158.
8. Inge, *Christian Mysticism*, Appendix B, "The Greek Mysteries and Christian Mysticism," p. 354. Inge's list does not include our first item.
9. Ibid., Appendix C, "The Doctrines of Deification," p. 358.

10. Benjamin Jowett, ed., *The Dialogues of Plato* (New York: Random House, 1937); Richard McKeon, ed., *The Basic Works of Aristotle* (New York: Random House, 1941); and Joseph Katz, trans., *The Philosophy of Plotinus* (New York: Appleton-Century-Crofts, 1950) are the sources from which the following discussion of these authors is drawn.
11. Katz, *The Philosophy of Plotinus,* p. 9.
12. Ibid., pp. 14-15.
13. Ibid., p. 15.
14. Ibid., pp. 143-44.
15. Ibid., p. 4.
16. Ibid., p. 156.
17. Quoted in Dom Cuthbert Butler, *Western Mysticism* (New York: Harper Torchbooks, 1966) p. 6.
18. C. E. Rolt, trans., *Dionysius The Areopagite on the Divine Names and the Mystical Theology* (New York: The Macmillan Co., 1951), p. 195.
19. Ibid., pp. 198-99.
20. Ibid., pp. 200-201.
21. St. John of the Cross, *Spiritual Canticle,* st. 38, E. Allison Peers, ed., *The Complete Works of St. John of the Cross* (Westminster, Md.: Newman Press, 1953), II, 168.
22. Augustine, *On Free Will* II, iii, 7. Quoted in J. H. S. Burleigh, ed., *Augustine: Earlier Writings,* The Library of Christian Classics (Philadelphia: Westminster Press, 1953), VI, 138.

Chapter 4

1. Blakney, Raymond B. trans., *Meister Eckhart* (New York: Harper & Brothers, 1941), p. 106.
2. Ibid., p. xxii.
3. Ibid., p. 219.
4. Ibid., p. 221.
5. Ibid., p. 85. Fortunately, Eckhart is not always consistent. Elsewhere he says that if to be comforted by a friend is to have one's misery "diminished by the sympathy of a friend," "how much more shall I find comfort in the companion of God!" (Blakney, *Meister Eckhart,* p. 67).
6. Ibid., p. 121.
7. Ibid., p. 54; see also p. 181.
8. See Blakney, p. 296, for Eckhart's defense of the sentence "He must do so whether he will or not," to be found in Blakney, p. 181.
9. Ibid., pp. 6, 53, 85.
10. Ibid., p. 127
11. Ibid., pp. 210, 74. Some of his other names for the inner kernel are: "castle" (or "ground") of the soul, "Tabernacle of the spirit," "light of the spirit," and "aristocrat of the soul."
12. Ibid., p. 211.
13. Ibid., pp. 103, 109
14. Ibid., pp. 180, 28-29, 29, 194.
15. Ibid., p. 207.
16. Ibid., pp. 97, 99.
17. Ibid., p. 119. The word that is translated as "unconsciousness" is *unwissen,* literally, "unknowledge," See Blakney, p. 317n.

18. Ibid., pp. 100, 114, 169.
19. Ibid., pp. 17, 205.
20. Ibid., pp. 136-37.
21. See especially Ernst Troeltsch, *The Social Teaching of the Christian Churches* (New York, The Macmillan Co., 1931), II, 730. See discussion pp. 729-802.
22. Blakney, *Meister Eckhart*, pp. 9, 116.
23. Ibid., pp. 127, 198.
24. Paul Tillich, *The Courage To Be* (New Haven: Yale University Press, 1952), pp. 182-90, 184-85, 187.
25. Blakney, *Meister Eckhart,* p. 229.
26. Here we do an injustice to Plotinus, who drew not one circle but several concentric circles, or "hypostases," and drew boundaries, not with the precision of a map maker but with the delicate shading and overlapping of an artist using soft pastels. The mystics, however, oversimplified him—and that is just our point.
27. Franz Pfeiffer, ed., *Meister Eckhart*, trans. C. DeB. Evans (London: John M. Watkins, 1924), p. 304; see also p. 128.
28. Blakney, Meister Eckhart, p. 228.
29. Edgar Allison Peers, ed., *The Way of Perfection and the Interior Castle*, vol. II, *The Complete Works of Saint Teresa of Avila* (New York and London: Sheed & Ward, 1957), p. 76.
30. David Lewis, trans., *The Life of St. Teresa of Avila, Including the Relations of Her Spiritual State, Written by Herself* (Westminster, Md.: The Newman Press, 1962), p. 283.
31. Ibid.
32. Peers, *The Interior Castle*, p. 202.
33. Lewis, *Life of St. Teresa*, pp. 122, 34.
34. Edgar Allison Peers, *Spanish Mysticism* (London: Methuen Co., 1924), p. 99.
35. Ibid., pp. 99, 100.
36. Ibid., p. 99; Lewis, *Life of St. Teresa*, p. 4.
37. Peers, *Spanish Mysticism*, p. 100.
38. Ibid.
39. Peers, *The Way of Perfection*, pp. 19-20; Lewis, *Life of St. Teresa*, p. 88.
40. Peers, *The Way of Perfection*, p. 45.
41. Lewis, *Life of St. Teresa*, p. 272.
42. Ibid., p. 69.
43. Ibid., p. 70.
44. Ibid., p. 78.
45. Peers, *The Way of Perfection*, p. 126.
46. Lewis, *Life of St. Teresa*, p. 92; Peers, *The Way of Perfection*, p. 129.
47. Lewis, *Life of St. Teresa*, pp. 107, 108.
48. Ibid., p. 110.
49. Ibid., p. 69.
50. Ibid., p. 119.
51. Ibid., p. 403.
52. Ibid., p. 222.
53. Ibid., p. 239.
54. Ibid., p. 225-26.
55. Blakney, *Meister Eckhart*, p. 20.

56. When God brings someone to the knowledge "of the fact that another world (*or*, let us say, another kingdom) exists, and that there is a great difference between the one and the other, the one being eternal and the other only a dream; and of what it is to love the Creator and what to love the creature (this must be discovered by experience, for it is a very different matter from merely thinking about it and believing it); . . . then one loves very differently from those of us who have not advanced thus far" (Peers, *The Way of Perfection*, p. 27).

57. Ibid., *The Interior Castle*, pp. 255-56. A strangely mixed metaphor.

Chapter 5

1. Ray C. Petry, ed., *Late Medieval Mysticism*, The Library of Christian Classics, vol. XIII (Philadelphia: The Westminster Press, 1957), p. 64; Friedrich von Hügel, *The Mystical Element of Religion as Studied in Saint Catherine of Genoa and Her Friends*, (London: J. M. Dent & Co., 1923) I, 159; Lewis, *The Life of St. Teresa of Avila, Including the Relations of Her Spiritual State, Written by Herself* (Westminster, Md: The Newman Press, 1962), p. 122.

2. Quoted in Lincoln Barnett, *The Universe and Dr. Einstein* (New York: Time-Life Books, 1962), p. 100.

3. William James, *The Varieties of Religious Experience* (New York: Collier Books, 1961), p. 299.

4. Evelyn Underhill, *Mysticism* (New York: Meridian Books, World Publishing Co., 1955) p. 444.

5. James, *Varieties of Religious Experience*, p. 355.

6. Dom Cuthbert Butler, *Western Mysticism* (New York: Harper Torchbooks, 1966), p. 128.

7. See the words of warning in Karl Barth's introductory essay to Ludwig Feuerbach's *Essence of Christianity*, trans. George Elliott (New York: Harper Torchbooks, 1957), pp. x-xxx.

8. William Ralph Inge, "Institutionalism and Mysticism" in *Outspoken Essays*, 2 vols. (New York: Longmans, Green & Co., 1927), I, 230-31.

9. Quoted in John Ratte, *Three Modernists* (London: Sheed & Ward, 1968), p. 20.

10. William E. Hocking, *Types of Philosophy*, (New York: Charles Scribner's Sons, 1959), p. 259.

11. Ibid., p. 272.

12. Ralph Barton Perry, *The Thought and Character of William James: Briefer Version* (New York: George Braziller, 1954), p. 364.

13. Ibid., p. 175.

14. James, *Varieties of Religious Experience*, p. 356.

15. Ibid., p. 42.

16. Ibid., p. 133.

17. Ibid., p. 220.

18. Ibid., p. 229.

19. Ibid., p. 335.

20. Ibid., p. 305.

Chapter 6

1. Rudolf Otto, *The Idea of the Holy*, trans. John W. Harvey (New York: Oxford University Press, 1958), p. xiii.
2. William Ralph Inge, *Outspoken Essays*, 2 vols. (New York: Longmans, Green & Co., 1927), I, ix, 30.
3. Ibid., pp. 121, 134.
4. Friedrich von Hügel, *The Mystical Element of Religion as Studied in Saint Catherine of Genoa and Her Friends*, 2nd ed., 2 vols. (London: J. M. Dent & Co., 1923), I, viii.
5. Von Hügel: "Indeed, even Professor James's in many respects valuable *Varieties of Religious Experience* is seriously damaged by a cognate tendency to treat Religion, or at least Mysticism, as an abnormal faculty for perceiving phenomena inexplicable by physical and psychical science" (*Mystical Element of Religion*, II, 308).
   Inge: "It is not surprising that these writers [like James, who begin with the psychological issues] collect mainly abnormal and even pathological cases, leaving the impression that they are dealing with a rare and probably unhealthy condition of the human mind" (*Christian Mysticism* [London: Methuen & Co., 1948], p. viii).
6. Evelyn Underhill, *Mysticism* (New York: Meridian Books, World Publishing Co., 1955) pp. vii, xv.
7. Ibid., pp. 24, 72.
8. Ibid., pp. 81-92.
9. Ibid., pp. 82, 81, 83, 82.
10. Ibid., p. 84.
11. Ibid., p. 84.
12. Ibid., pp. 84, 70, 71.
13. Ibid., pp. 85, 81.
14. Ibid., p. 85.
15. Ibid., pp. 90, 81.
16. Ibid., pp. 176-265, 413-43.
17. Ibid., p. 413.
18. Ibid., pp. 308-9.
19. Ibid., p. 310.
20. Ibid., p. 95.
21. Ibid., pp. 102, 455.
22. Ibid., p. 445.
23. William Ralph Inge, *Mysticism in Religion* (The University of Chicago Press, 1948), p. 9.
24. Inge, *Christian Mysticism*, p. 5.
25. Ibid., p. 87.
26. Ibid., pp. 10, 11, 12.
27. Inge, *Outspoken Essays*, II, p. 50.
28. Inge, *Christian Mysticism*, p. 143.
29. Ibid., p. 217.
30. Inge, *Mysticism in Religion*, p. 8; *Outspoken Essays*, I, 192; *Christian Mysticism*, pp. 340-41.
31. Ibid., p. 5.
32. Inge, *Outspoken Essays*, II, p. 59; I, 242.
33. Inge, *Christian Mysticism*, pp. 212, 119.

34. William Ralph Inge, *Personal Idealism and Mysticism* (London: Longmans, Green, & Co., 1907), pp. 99, 102, 120-21; *Christian Mysticism*, p. 340.
35. Ibid., pp. 30, 31.
36. Von Hügel, *Mystical Element of Religion*, I, 50-82.
37. Friedrich von Hügel, *Essays and Addresses on the Philosophy of Religion*, 2 vols. (London: J. M. Dent & Co., 1921–26) II, 240; *Mystical Element of Religion*, II, 267.
38. Von Hügel, *Essays and Addresses*, I, 279.
39. Ibid., II, 198-99.

Chapter 7

1. Martin Buber, *I and Thou*, trans. Walter Kaufmann (New York: Charles Scribner's Sons, 1970), p. 63.
2. Ibid., p. 131.
3. Brunner, however, disavowed any direct borrowing from Buber. The conception of I-Thou begins with Ludwig Feuerbach and Ferdinand Ebner. See "Afterword, The History of the Dialogical Principle" in Buber, *Between Man and Man* (New York: The Macmillan Co., 1966), pp. 209-24.
4. Emil Brunner, *The Mediator* (Philadelphia: The Westminster Press, 1947), pp. 278, 279.
5. Emil Brunner, *Revelation and Reason* (Philadelphia: The Westminster Press, 1946), p. 33.
6. Brunner, *The Mediator*, pp. 279, 110.
7. Emil Brunner, *The Divine Imperative* (Philadelphia: The Westminster Press, 1947), pp. 111, 134-35.
8. Brunner, *The Mediator*, p. 119.
9. Ibid., p. 527.
10. Ibid.
11. At several points, Brunner implies rather than fully develops the distinction between his own use of paradox and that of the mystics'. See his *Christian Doctrine of God* (Philadelphia: The Westminster Press, 1950), pp. 118, 179; *Man in Revolt* (Philadelphia: The Westminster Press, 1947), p. 437; *Revelation and Reason*, p. 45.
12. Brunner, *The Divine Imperative*, pp. 129, 306.
13. Ibid., p. 208.
14. Ibid., p. 327.
15. See especially Rudolf Otto on the "Means by Which the Numinous Is Expressed in Art" in *The Idea of The Holy* (Oxford University Press, 1958), pp. 65-71.
16. Pseudo-Dionysius in Dom Cuthbert Butler, *Western Mysticism* (New York: Harper Torchbooks, 1966), p. 6; Raymond B. Blakney, trans., *Meister Eckhart* (New York: Harper & Brothers, 1941), p. 114.
17. Joseph Katz, trans., *The Philosophy of Plotinus* (New York: Appleton-Century-Crofts, 1950), p. 156; Meister Eckhart in Aldous Huxley, *The Perennial Philosophy* (New York: Harper & Row Colophon, 1970), p. 12.
18. St. Catherine of Genoa, Eckhart, *The Perennial Philosophy*, pp. 11, 12.
19. David Lewis, trans., *The Life of St. Teresa of Avila, Including the*

Relations of Her Spiritual State, Written by Herself (Westminster, Md.: The Newman Press, 1962), p. 161.

20. Anselm in the preface to the *Proslogium*. See Sidney Norton Deane, trans., *St. Anselm* (LaSalle, Illinois: Open Court, 1958), p. 1.

21. One issue in any appraisal of the use of drugs and other devices to induce mystical experience is whether the means used can or should become technologically efficient if the ultimate aim is the abandonment of all means.

22. The difficulty with accepting "visions" of Jesus, the devil, et cetera, as evidence is that it places the mystic's world view *within* the empirical boundary instead of showing it as a vista that comes into view *on* the boundary of "this world" and "that world." The vista cannot simply be made a datum of empirical experience.

23. Both Buber and Brunner see the necessity of "its" but neither can quite find them desirable. Buber: "Every You in the world is doomed by its nature to become a thing." "One cannot live in the pure present. . . . In all the seriousness of truth, listen: without It a human being cannot live. But whoever lives only with that is not human" (*I and Thou,* pp. 69, 85).

24. Swami Prabhavananda and Christopher Isherwood, trans., *The Song of God: Bhagavad-Gita* (New York: Mentor Books, New American Library, 1944), p. 123.

25. Arthur Waley, *The Way and Its Power: A Study of the Tao Tê Ching and Its Place in Chinese Thought* (New York: Grove Press, 1951), p. 165.

26. Gabriel Marcel gives a personal example: "I promised C—— the other day that I would come back to the nursing home where he has been dying for weeks, and see him again. This promise seemed to me, when I made it, to spring from the inmost depths of my being. A promise moved by a wave of pity: he is doomed, he knows it, he knows I know it. Several days have gone by since my visit. The circumstances which dictated my promise are unchanged; I have no room for self-deception about that. I should be able to say—yes, I even dare assert—that he still inspires the same compassion in me. How could I justify a change in the state of my feelings, since nothing has happened since which could have the power to alter them? And yet I must in honesty admit that the pity I *felt* the other day, is today no more than a theoretical pity. I still judge that he is unhappy and that it is right to be sorry for him, but this is a judgment I should not have dreamed of formulating the other day. There was no need. My whole being was concentrated into an irresistible impulse toward him, a wild longing to help him, to show him that I was on his side, that his sufferings were mine. I have to recognize that this impulse no longer exists, and it is no longer in my power to do more than imitate it by a pretence which some part of me refuses to swallow. All that I can do is to observe that C—— is unhappy and alone and that I cannot let him down; also, I have promised to come back; my signature is at the foot of the bond and the bond is in his possession" (*Being and Having* [New York: Harper Torchbooks, 1965], pp. 47-48).

Indexes

Index of Scripture

Index of Selected Anecdotes and Quotations

Index of Subjects